IN RECITAL™
Throughout the Year
(with Performance Strategies)
Volume Two

ABOUT THE SERIES • A NOTE TO THE TEACHER

In Recital ™ — *Throughout the Year* is a series that focuses on fabulous repertoire, intended to motivate your students. We know that to motivate, the teacher must challenge the student with attainable goals. This series makes that possible. The fine composers and arrangers of this series have created musically engaging pieces, which have been carefully leveled and address the technical strengths and weaknesses of students. The wide range of styles in each book of the series complements other FJH publications and will help you to plan students' recital repertoire for the entire year. You will find original solos and duets that focus on different musical and technical issues, giving you the selection needed to accommodate your students' needs. There are arrangements of famous classical themes, as well as repertoire written for Halloween, Christmas, and Fourth of July recitals. In this way, your student will have recital pieces throughout the entire year! Additionally, the series provides a progressive discussion on the art of performance. The earlier levels offer tips on recital preparation, while the later levels address more advanced technical and psychological issues that help to realize successful performances.

 Use the enclosed CD as a teaching and motivational tool. Have your students listen to the recording and discuss interpretation with you!

Production: Frank and Gail Hackinson
Production Coordinators: Philip Groeber and Isabel Otero Bowen
Cover: Terpstra Design, San Francisco
Cover Piano Illustration: Keith Criss
Engraving: Kevin Olson and Tempo Music Press, Inc.
Printer: Tempo Music Press, Inc.

ISBN 1-56939-478-4

9 RECITAL PREPARATION TIPS • FOR THE TEACHER

1. Consider a tiered approach to developing comfort in performance. Make "mini" performances a regular occurrence, probably without even calling them performances. Have a student play for the student who follows his/her lesson. It doesn't matter if their leveling is different; the older students are naturally nice to the young and the young provide a non-threatening audience for the older. Have students play mini concerts at home. Younger students may enjoy concerts for their favorite stuffed animals each day after practice. Advise older students to practice performing by recording themselves. Of course, you will tailor these suggestions according to each student's personality. Just remember, *no venue is too small and frequency is the key.* Suggestions for mini-performances and performance strategies are also addressed on pages 20, 21, and 35.

   Once students are comfortable with these "mini" performances, teachers must create opportunities for students to play in public, so that they will get used to the idea of getting up on stage and playing for others. Studio group lessons or performance classes are perfect for trial performances, then take it to the next step and invite family or friends to a performance class.

   Try these different performance venues and you will be pleased with the results. The "tiered" approach helps performance to become a natural part of piano study.

2. Make sure that your students have the opportunity to perform pieces well within their technical range. These performances will help build student confidence and will make a huge difference when they are playing more challenging repertoire.

3. Have students practice concentrating on the tempo, mood, and dynamics of the piece before beginning to play.

4. Coach students on how to walk purposefully *to* the piano, adjust the bench, and check their position relative to the piano. Have them practice this a lot in the lesson and at home. Familiarity with the process really helps.

5. Talk to your students about how to finish the piece. Coach them to stay with the music until the piece is over. Discuss how they will move at the end of the piece: i.e., quickly moving the hands away from the keyboard, or slowly lifting the hands with the lifting of the pedal, depending on the repertoire.

6. Coach students how to bow and walk purposefully *away* from the piano. Again, practice this together often so that it feels natural to them.

7. Remind students to keep the recital in perspective. The recital piece should be one of several the student is working on, so that they understand that there is "life after the recital."

8. If possible, have a practice session in the performance location. Encourage your students to focus on what they can control and remind them that although a piano may feel differently, their technique will not "go away."

9. Have your students listen to the companion CD. Not only does this give them ideas on how to interpret the pieces, it builds an intuitive knowledge of how the pieces sound, which helps increase confidence and comfort.

The goal is to instill in our students the excitement of playing for others and to demystify the process. There is nothing quite like communicating a piece of music to an audience and then enjoying their positive reaction to it. With our help, our students can perform up to their potential in public and enjoy this exciting and rewarding experience.

ORGANIZATION OF THE SERIES
IN RECITAL™ • THROUGHOUT THE YEAR

*I*n Recital™ — *Throughout the Year* is carefully leveled into the following six categories: Early Elementary, Elementary, Late Elementary, Early Intermediate, Intermediate, and Late Intermediate. Each of the works has been selected for its artistic as well as its pedagogical merit.

Book Five — Intermediate, reinforces the following concepts:

■ Triplet and sixteenth-note patterns are used, as well as ♩. ♪ rhythmic patterns and syncopated rhythms.

■ Students play one and two octave scale passages and blocked octaves.

■ Students play rolled chords and double third configurations.

■ Students play pieces with *rubato*.

■ Chords and their inversions are reinforced.

■ Students play two voices within the same hand.

■ Simple ornamentation is used.

■ Pieces introduce the following musical terms: *cantabile*, *largamente*, *molto agitato*, along with basic musical terminology found in books 1-4.

■ A mixture of major and minor keys strengthen a student's command of the piano.

In addition to the solo pieces in this book, there are two equal part duets: *Distant Dream*, and *The Barber of Seville*.

TABLE OF CONTENTS

	Recital Category	Composer	Arranger	Page	CD Track
9 Recital Preparation Tips — For the Teacher	by Helen Marlais			2	
Canto de Estío (Song of Summer)	Lyrical Solo	Martín Cuéllar		6	1
Dance Masquerade	Showpiece Solo	Timothy Brown		10	2
Distant Dream	Equal Part Duet	David Karp		14	3
Calendar for Success	by Helen Marlais			20	
The Barber of Seville Overture	Classical Theme Equal Part Duet	Gioachino Antonio Rossini	Timothy Brown	22	4
We Wish You a Jazzy Christmas	Christmas Solo	Traditional English Carol	Edwin McLean	26	5
Presto	Showpiece Solo	Valerie Roth Roubos		29	6
Serenade	Lyrical Solo	Melody Bober		32	7
Practicing with the Metronome	by Helen Marlais			35	
Miniature Overture from *The Nutcracker Suite*, Op. 71a	Classical Theme Solo	Peter Ilyich Tchaikovsky	Kevin Olson	36	8
About the Composers/Arrangers				39	

to Margaret S. Wyckoff

CANTO DE ESTÍO
(Song of Summer)

Martín Cuéllar

Dance Masquerade

Timothy Brown

to Dr. Helen Marlais

DISTANT DREAM
Secondo

David Karp

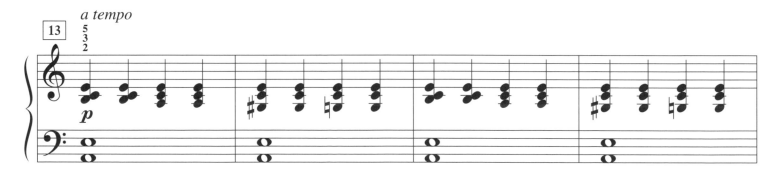

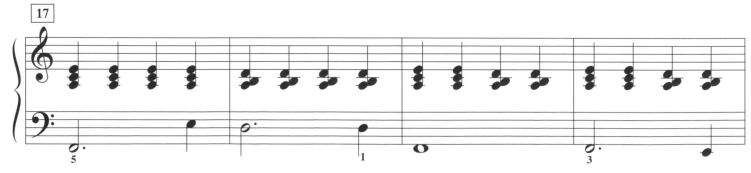

to Dr. Helen Marlais

DISTANT DREAM
Primo

David Karp

FF1556

Secondo

Primo

Secondo

Primo

 ith your teacher, set your "Calendar for Success."

SU	M	T	W	TH	F	S

Write on the line below the date of your recital:

_____

1 GOAL #1: Write the date you will have your piece *memorized* for performance (this should be at least four weeks before the recital):

_____

In order for GOAL #1 to become a reality, goals #2, #3, and #4 must be met.

2 GOAL #2: Write the date when you will have learned your entire piece with 100% accuracy in regard to notes, rhythms, and fingerings:

_____

3 GOAL #3: Write the date you will be able to play your piece *up to tempo*:

_____

4 GOAL #4: Write the date you will be able to play your piece as an artistic performance. This is the date you will be able to pay attention to all of the details that make your interpretation of the piece effective:

_____

(This last goal can be done before or after Goal #1 is achieved.)

You can use these two pages as a practice guide for every recital piece you play in this book!

BEFORE THE RECITAL

It's exciting to play a recital! In order to be able to play with enthusiasm, confidence, and energy, follow these performance strategies:

1. Set a performance time every day and play your repertoire piece(s) straight through, without stopping. This performance strategy helps your body and mind remember what it has to do on performance day.

2. Can you play the piece with your eyes closed? (Make a habit of *performing* with your eyes *open*, but closing your eyes is a good test.)

3. Practice your recital piece(s) without any pedal, to make sure you are playing the rhythms completely accurately and that your timing is perfect!

4. The night before, get a good night sleep. You will need energy for the performance!

THE DAY OF THE RECITAL

Many performers have a routine that they follow. Here are some routines you can try!

- Warm up slowly.

- Underplay, not overplay. "Underplaying" means to practice only a short period of time, so that you don't play so much that you are tired for the recital!

- Your performance is like a tennis match, although your opponent is you. You are competing against your very best self. So, it is important to be positive and feel that you can go out on stage and play well because you have prepared well!

- To play or not to play the day of a performance is a question that every pianist thinks about. Every musician is different; some find security in practicing. Others will not touch the piano until it is performance time. It is always a good idea to warm up but you can choose to warm up on something other than your recital piece.

- You can choose to play your recital piece up to tempo *before* the recital, or wait to play it up to tempo *at* the recital.

For suggestions on **Practicing With the Metronome,** turn to page 35.

The Barber of Seville

Overture

Secondo

Gioachino Antonio Rossini
arr. Timothy Brown

Allegro (♩ = ca. 138)

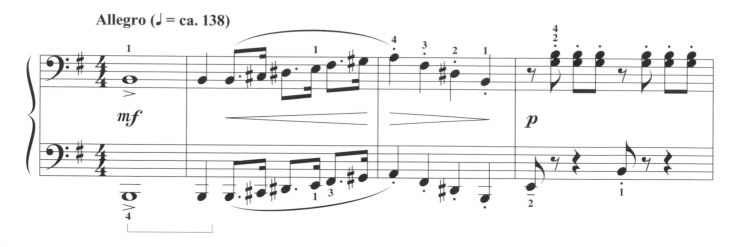

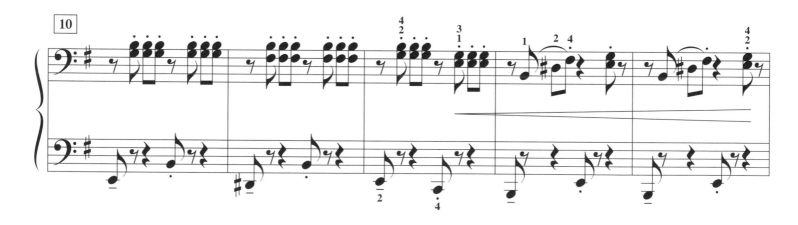

THE BARBER OF SEVILLE
Overture
Primo

Gioachino Antonio Rossini
arr. Timothy Brown

Allegro (♩ = ca. 138)

FF1556

Secondo

Primo

WE WISH YOU A JAZZY CHRISTMAS

Traditional English Carol
arr. Edwin McLean

With an easy swing (♩ = 116-126) (♫ = ♪³♪)

PRESTO

Valerie Roth Roubos

Molto agitato (♩ = ca. 160)

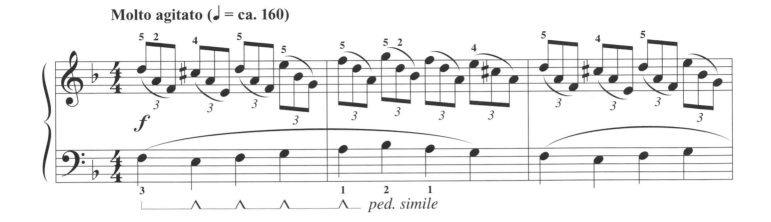

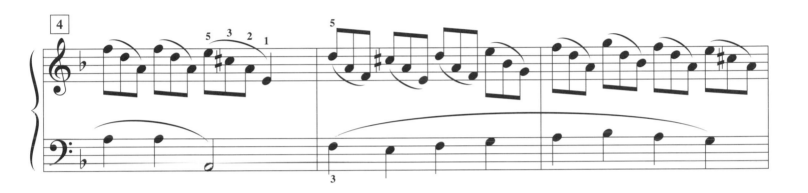

FF1556

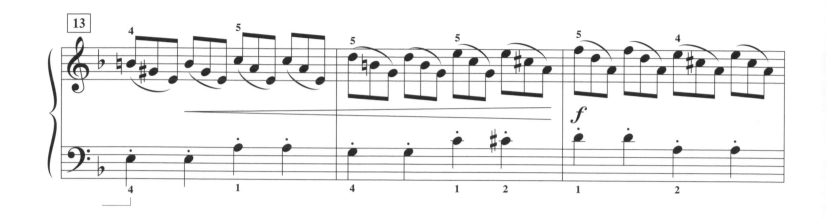

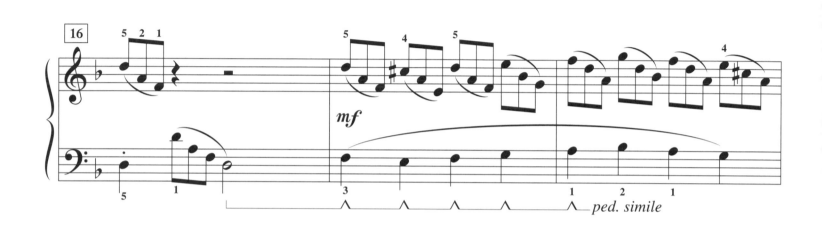

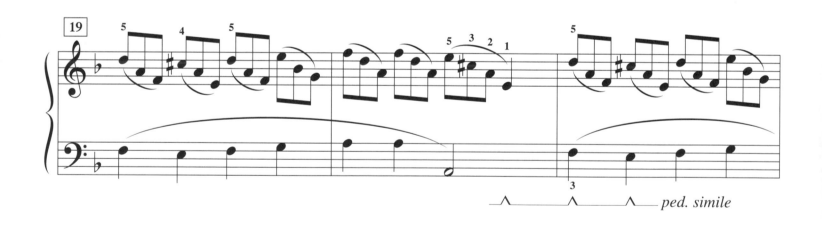

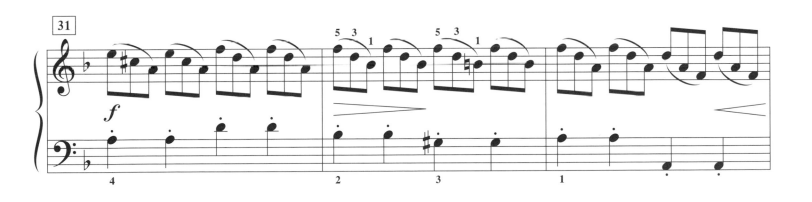

Serenade

Melody Bober

PRACTICING WITH THE METRONOME

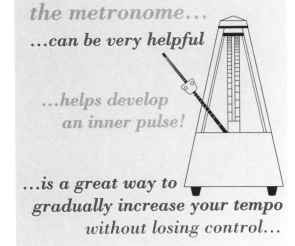

the metronome...

...can be very helpful

...helps develop an inner pulse!

...is a great way to gradually increase your tempo without losing control...

The metronome can be very helpful; with it, you can make sure that you are playing in tempo. The metronome helps develop an inner pulse!

———— The metronome is a great way to gradually increase your tempo without losing control.

———— Using this checklist, check off each of these practice strategies every day. Start at least four weeks before your recital.

WITH THE METRONOME:

———— **Practice** beginnings, endings, and all transitions.

———— **Play** one hand and then every once in a while try to bring in the other hand without stopping. This is difficult to do at first but then gets easier with practice.

———— **Count** your entire piece aloud. Keep going to the end of the piece, no matter what happens. You will find that counting the beats keeps you focused and steadier than you could ever imagine!

———— **With your metronome** set at a much slower tempo, practice your entire recital piece in a detached style, being sure to play to the *bottom* of the keys with a big, warm sound.

———— **Start** your piece at four *different* places in the music. (You and your teacher can pick four good starting places).

———— **Practice** the piece from beginning to end at "half tempo." ("Half tempo" means to play it with all of the correct rhythms, notes, and dynamics, but at half of the speed you would play it when performing it.)

Once you can play your piece and stay with the metronome from beginning to end steadily many times for several weeks, then you may turn off your metronome, play more freely, and add musical elements such as *ritardando* and *rubato*, as you can easily hear on the CD recording.

> You can use this page as a practice guide for every recital piece you play in this book!

MINIATURE OVERTURE

from *The Nutcracker Suite*, Op. 71a

Peter Ilyich Tchaikovsky
arr. Kevin Olson

ABOUT THE COMPOSERS/ARRANGERS

Melody Bober

Piano instructor, music teacher, composer, clinician—Melody Bober has been active in music education for over 25 years. As a composer, her goal is to create exciting and challenging pieces that are strong teaching tools to promote a lifelong love, understanding, and appreciation for music. Pedagogy, ear training, and musical expression are fundamentals of Melody's teaching, as well as fostering composition skills in her students.

Melody graduated with highest honors from the University of Illinois with a degree in music education, and later received a master's degree in piano performance. She maintains a large private studio, performs in numerous regional events, and conducts workshops across the country. She and her husband Jeff reside in Minnesota.

Timothy Brown

Composition has always been a natural form of self-expression for Timothy Brown. His Montessori-influenced philosophy has greatly helped define his approach as a teacher and composer of educational music. His composition originates from a love of improvisation at the piano and his personal goal of writing music that will help release the student's imagination.

Mr. Brown holds two degrees in piano performance, including a master's degree from the University of North Texas. His many honors include a "Commissioned for Clavier" magazine article, and first prize award in the Fifth Aliénor International Harpsichord Competition for his solo composition *Suite Española*. As a clinician, Mr. Brown has presented numerous clinics and most recently represented FJH Music with his presentation at the 2000 World Piano Pedagogy Conference. Currently living in Dallas, Mr. Brown teaches piano and composition at the Harry Stone Montessori Magnet School. He frequently serves as an adjudicator for piano and composition contests, and performs with his wife as duo-pianists.

Martín Cuéllar

Pianist Martín Cuéllar is Assistant Professor of Piano at Emporia State University in Emporia, Kansas. He received his Doctor of Musical Arts and Master of Music degrees in piano performance from The University of Texas at Austin. As a rotary scholar, Dr. Cuéllar studied at The Royal Conservatory of Music in Madrid, Spain, where he received the diploma in piano performance. He has done additional research and piano studies on the music of Enrique Granados at the Marshall Academy of Music in Barcelona, Spain. His edition of Enrique Granados' Valses Poéticos, published by The FJH Music Company, enjoys universal, critical acclaim.

An active performer, Dr. Cuéllar plays concerts throughout the United States, Mexico, Brazil, and Spain. He is a member of the National Guild of Piano Teachers, chair of the guild's International Piano Composition Contest, and adjudicator for the organization both nationally and internationally. Many of his piano compositions are on the required repertoire list of the National Federation of Music Clubs. Martín Cuéllar currently resides in Emporia, Kansas, with his wife and two children.

David Karp

Dr. David Karp—nationally known pianist, composer, and educator—holds degrees from Manhattan School of Music and the University of Colorado. He has also done graduate work at Teachers College, Columbia University. Dr. Karp is currently professor of music at SMU's Meadows School of the Arts and director of the National Piano Teachers Institute.

As a clinician and adjudicator, Dr. Karp has traveled the United States from Alaska to New Hampshire, as well as internationally. He has been a guest conductor and commissioned composer for the New Hampshire Summer Piano Camp at Plymouth State University, and was recently honored with the establishment of the David Karp Piano Festival, which is held each spring at Kilgore College. In June 2002, Dr. Karp served on the panel of judges for the Van Cliburn International Piano Competition for Outstanding Amateurs.

40

Edwin McLean

Edwin McLean is a freelance composer living in Chapel Hill, North Carolina. He is a graduate of the Yale School of Music, where he studied with Krzysztof Penderecki and Jacob Druckman. He also holds a master's degrees in music theory and a bachelor's degree in piano performance from the University of Colorado.

The recipient of several grants and awards: The MacDowell Colony, the John Work Award, the Woods Chandler Prize (Yale), Meet the Composer, Florida Arts Council, and others, he has also won the Aliénor Composition Competition for his work *Sonata for Harpsichord*, published by The FJH Music Company and recorded by Elaine Funaro (*Into the Millennium*, Gasparo GSCD-331).

Since 1979, Edwin McLean has arranged the music of some of today's best known recording artists. Currently, he is senior editor as well as MIDI orchestrator for FJH Music.

Kevin Olson

Kevin Olson is an active pianist, composer, and faculty member at Elmhurst College near Chicago, Illinois, where he teaches classical and jazz piano, music theory, and electronic music. He holds a Doctor of Education degree from National-Louis University, and bachelor's and master's degrees in music composition and theory from Brigham Young University. Before teaching at Elmhurst College, he held a visiting professor position at Humboldt State University in California.

A native of Utah, Kevin began composing at the age of five. When he was twelve, his composition *An American Trainride* received the Overall First Prize at the 1983 National PTA Convention in Albuquerque, New Mexico. Since then, he has been a composer-in-residence at the National Conference on Piano Pedagogy and has written music for the American Piano Quartet, Chicago a cappella, the Rich Matteson Jazz Festival, among others. Kevin maintains a large piano studio, teaching students of a variety of ages and abilities. Many of the needs of his own piano students have inspired over forty books and solos published by The FJH Music Company Inc., which he joined as a writer in 1994.

Valerie Roth Roubos

Valerie Roth Roubos is a graduate of the University of Wyoming, where she earned degrees in music theory and composition, and flute performance. She has taught flute and piano for the past fifteen years in her home in Spokane, Washington.

Valerie's teaching philosophy and compositions reflect her belief that all students, from elementary to advanced, are capable of playing music with sensitivity and expression. Her compositions represent a variety of musical styles, including sacred, choral, and educational piano works.

Ms. Roubos participates in several local and state music organizations in the Spokane area, where she is also an active performer and accompanist. In 2000, the South Dakota Music Teachers Association and MTNA commissioned her to write *An American Portrait*.

T0011632

IN RECITAL®
for the Advancing Pianist
Classical Themes

ABOUT THE SERIES

In Recital® for the Advancing Pianist—Classical Themes continues the ever-popular six-book *In Recital®* series by presenting artistic Classical themes for the early advanced pianist. Pianists will have the enjoyment of learning some of the finest themes by some of the greatest composers to have lived. The fine arrangers of this collection have created engaging arrangements of these timeless treasures. The wide variety of repertoire—encompassing works from the Baroque, Classical, and Romantic eras will certainly be enjoyable for pianists, day after day!

THE FJH MUSIC COMPANY INC.
Frank J. Hackinson

Production: Frank J. Hackinson
Production Coordinators: Joyce Loke and Satish Bhakta
Cover Design: Terpstra Design, San Francisco, CA
Cover Art Concept: Helen Marlais
Cover Illustration: Keith Criss
Engraving: Tempo Music Press, Inc.
Printer: Tempo Music Press, Inc.

ISBN-13: 978-1-56939-832-6

TABLE OF CONTENTS

	Composer	Arranger	Page
Jesu, Joy of Man's Desiring from *Cantata No. 147*	Johann Sebastian Bach	Timothy Brown	4-7
Cello Concerto in C (*Movement One*)	Franz Joseph Haydn	Valerie Roth Roubos	8-11
Jupiter from *The Planets*	Gustav Holst	Chris Lobdell	12-14
Flower Duet from *Lakmé*	Leo Delibes	Robert Schultz	15-17
Symphony No. 4 (*Opus 120, No. 3, Scherzo*)	Robert Schumann	Valerie Roth Roubos	18-21
Romeo & Juliet Love Themes from the *Fantasy Overture*	Pyotr Ilyich Tchaikovsky	Chris Lobdell	22-25
Waltz from *Serenade for Strings*	Pyotr Ilyich Tchaikovsky	Robert Schultz	26-30
Shepherd's Song from *Symphony No. 6, Movement Five*	Ludwig van Beethoven	Timothy Brown	31-35
The Dance of the Hours from *La Gioconda*	Amilcare Ponchielli	Valerie Roth Roubos	36-38
Symphony No. 9 "From the New World" (*Opus 95, Movement Four*)	Antonín Dvořák	Robert Schultz	39-41
Symphony No. 4 (*Opus 90, Movement One*)	Felix Mendelssohn	Chris Lobdell	42-45
The Swan Lake Ballet (*Opus 20, Finale*)	Pyotr Ilyich Tchaikovsky	Timothy Brown	46-49
About the Arrangers			50-51

FJH2104

Jesu, Joy of Man's Desiring

from *Cantata No. 147*

Johann Sebastian Bach
arr. Timothy Brown

CELLO CONCERTO IN C

(Movement One)

Franz Joseph Haydn
arr. Valerie Roth Roubos

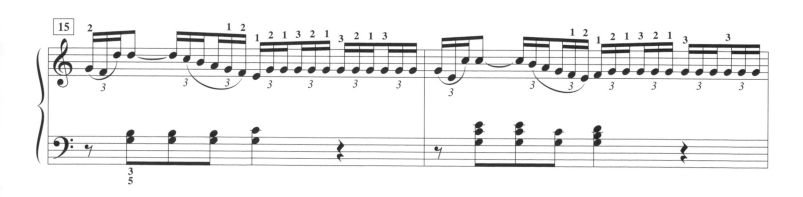

JUPITER
from *The Planets*

Gustav Holst
arr. Chris Lobdell

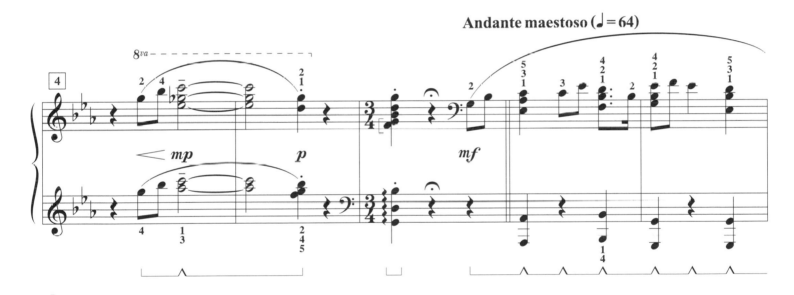

14

FLOWER DUET

from *Lakmé*

Leo Delibes
arr. Robert Schultz

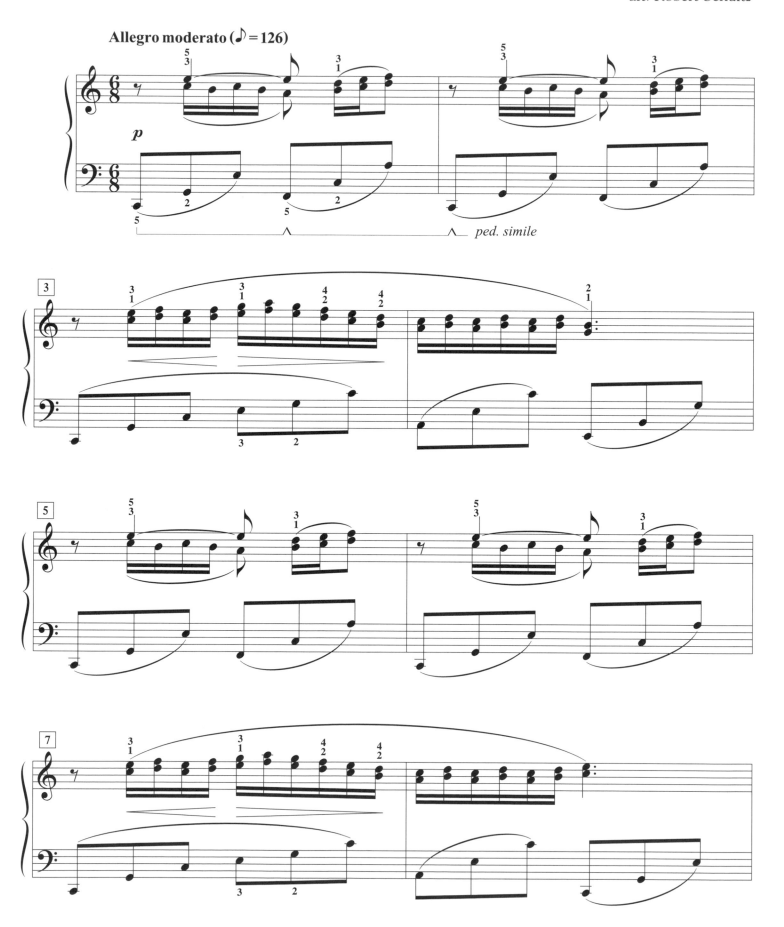

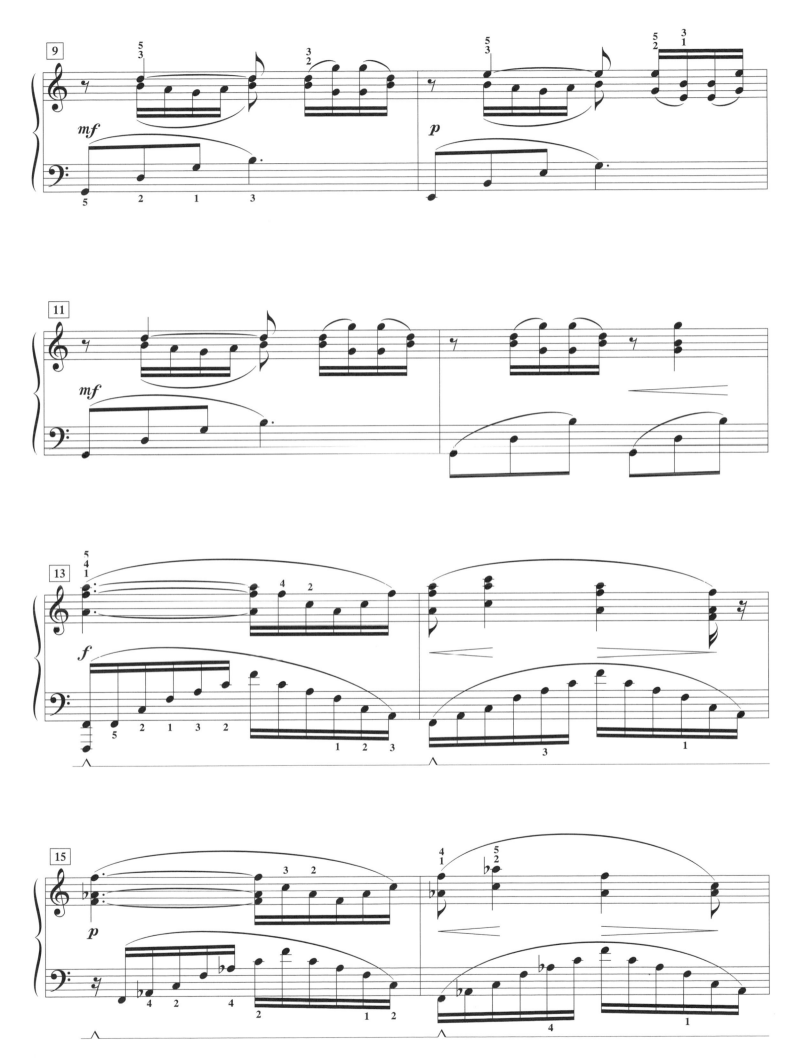

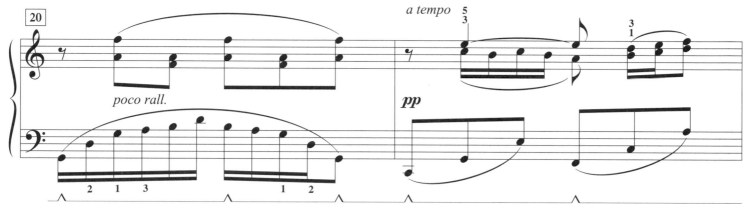

Symphony No. 4

(*Opus 120, No. 3, Scherzo*)

Robert Schumann
arr. Valerie Roth Roubos

ROMEO & JULIET

Love Themes from the *Fantasy Overture*

Pyotr Ilyich Tchaikovsky
arr. Chris Lobdell

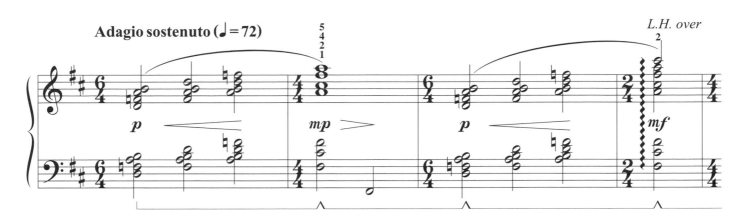

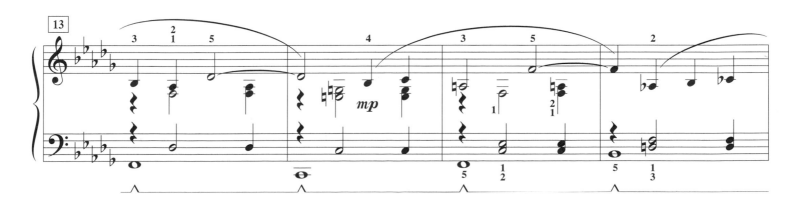

WALTZ

from *Serenade for Strings*

Pyotr Ilyich Tchaikovsky
arr. Robert Schultz

Tempo di Valse ($\dot{}$ = 69)

sempre legato

poco cresc.

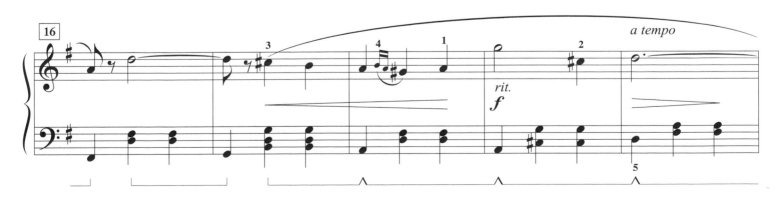

rit. *a tempo* *f*

Shepherd's Song

from *Symphony No. 6, Movement Five*

Ludwig van Beethoven
arr. Timothy Brown

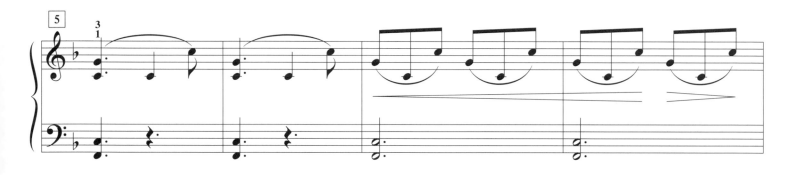

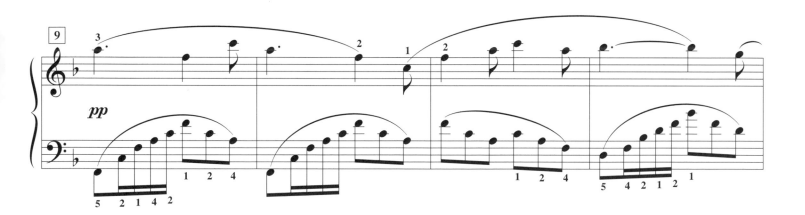

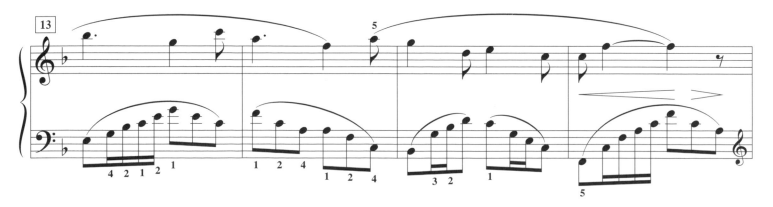

FJH2104

THE DANCE OF THE HOURS

from *La Gioconda*

Amilcare Ponchielli
arr. Valerie Roth Roubos

This arrangement © 2010 by The FJH Music Company Inc. (ASCAP).
International Copyright Secured.   Made in U.S.A.   All Rights Reserved.

SYMPHONY No. 9
"FROM THE NEW WORLD"
(Opus 95, Movement Four)

Antonín Dvořák
arr. Robert Schultz

Allegro con fuoco (♩ = 132)

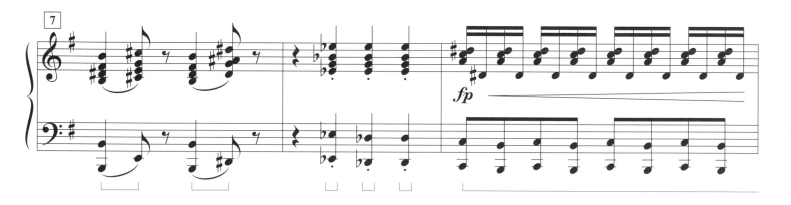

N.B. Bring out the melody in the inner voices in measures 10-16 and 44-49.

FJH2104

Symphony No. 4

(*Opus 90, Movement One*)

Felix Mendelssohn
arr. Chris Lobdell

44

THE SWAN LAKE BALLET

(Opus 20, Finale)

Pyotr Ilyich Tchaikovsky
arr. Timothy Brown

Moderato agitato (♩ = 92)

con pedale

ABOUT THE ARRANGERS

Timothy Brown

Timothy Brown holds a master's degree in piano performance from the University of North Texas, where he studied piano with Adam Wodnicki and music composition with Newel Kay Brown. He was later a recipient of a research fellowship from the Royal Holloway, University of London, where he performed postgraduate studies in music composition and orchestration, studying with English composer Brian Lock. His numerous credits as a composer include first prize at the Aliénor International Harpsichord Competition for his harpsichord solo *Suite Española* (Centaur Records). Mr. Brown leads a very active career as an exclusive composer and clinician for The FJH Music Company Inc.

Mr. Brown's works have been performed by concert artist Elaine Funaro on NPR, and most recently at the Spoleto Music Festival and the Library of Congress Concert Series in Washington, D.C. His numerous commissions include a commission by *Clavier* Magazine for his piano solo *Once Upon a Time*, edited by Denes Agay. Mr. Brown is currently a fine arts specialist for the Dallas Public Schools and serves on the advisory board of the Booker T. Washington High School for the Performing and Visual Arts in Dallas, Texas.

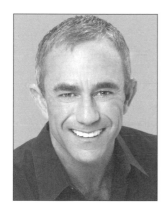

Chris Lobdell

Chris Lobdell, a native of Washington State, is nationally established as a composer-arranger, teacher, studio musician, pianist, and producer, whose compositions range from solo piano to full orchestral works. Chris has written and orchestrated for major symphony orchestras, full production shows for various cruise lines, film and video soundtracks for national television commercials, has created MIDI orchestration tracks for several piano series, and has ten years of experience as an MTNA-certified teacher. He continues an 18-year relationship with the music publishing industry as a composer, arranger, and orchestrator, and has over twenty-five books of piano arrangements in worldwide distribution.

In 1988, Chris received the U.S. President's Award for musical arrangements in the nationwide "Take Pride in America" campaign. He has served as a national adjudicator for American Guild of Music (AGM) competitions, and has been a featured presenter of technology workshops at the Florida state affiliate of MTNA and at the AGM national conference. In October of 2003, the Kirkland Orchestra commissioned Mr. Lobdell as orchestrator and featured pianist for the world premier of re-discovered works of Sergei Rachmaninoff, "Sophie's Songs."

ABOUT THE ARRANGERS

Valerie Roth Roubos

Valerie Roth Roubos earned degrees in music theory, composition, and flute performance from the University of Wyoming. Ms. Roubos maintains a studio in her home in Spokane, Washington, where she teaches flute, piano, and composition.

Active as a performer, adjudicator, lecturer, and accompanist, Ms. Roubos has lectured and taught master classes at the Washington State Music Teachers Conference, Holy Names Music Camp, and the Spokane and Tri-Cities chapters of Washington State Music Teachers Association. She has played an active role in the Spokane Music Teachers Association and WSMTA.

In 2001, the South Dakota Music Teachers Association selected Ms. Roubos as Composer of the Year, and with MTNA commissioned her to write *An American Portrait: Scenes from the Great Plains*, published by The FJH Music Company Inc. Ms. Roubos was chosen to be the 2004–2005 composer-in-residence at Washington State University. In 2006, WSMTA selected her as Composer of the Year.

Ms. Roubos' teaching philosophy and compositions reflect her belief that all students, from elementary to advanced, are capable of musical playing that incorporates sensitivity and expression. Her compositions represent a variety of musical styles, including sacred, choral, and educational piano works.

Robert Schultz

Robert Schultz, composer, arranger, and editor, has achieved international fame during his career in the music publishing industry. The Schultz Piano Library, established in 1980, has included more than 500 publications of classical works, popular arrangements, and Schultz's original compositions in editions for pianists of every level from the beginner through the concert artist. In addition to his extensive library of published piano works, Schultz's output includes original orchestral works, chamber music, works for solo instruments, and vocal music.

Schultz has presented his published editions at workshops, clinics, and convention showcases throughout the United States and Canada. He is a long-standing member of ASCAP and has served as president of the Miami Music Teachers Association. Mr. Schultz's original piano compositions and transcriptions are featured on the compact disc recordings *Visions of Dunbar* and *Tina Faigen Plays Piano Transcriptions*, released on the ACA Digital label and available worldwide. His published original works for concert artists are noted in Maurice Hinson's *Guide to the Pianist's Repertoire, Third Edition*. He currently devotes his full time to composing and arranging. In-depth information about Robert Schultz and The Schultz Piano Library is available at the Web site www.schultzmusic.com.

Write, Play, and Hear
Your Theory Every Day®

Helen Marlais with Peggy O'Dell and Kristen Avila

Production: Frank J. Hackinson
Production Coordinators: Joyce Loke and Satish Bhakta
Cover: Terpstra Design, San Francisco
Engraving: Tempo Music Press, Inc.
Printer: Tempo Music Press, Inc.

ISBN-13: 978-1-56939-744-2

ABOUT THE AUTHORS

Helen Marlais' active performance schedule includes collaborative concerts throughout North America, Europe, and Asia. Her travels abroad have included performing and teaching at the leading conservatories and festivals in Italy, France, Hungary, Turkey, Lithuania, Estonia, China, and England. Dr. Marlais has performed with members of the Chicago, Pittsburgh, Minnesota, Grand Rapids, Des Moines, Cedar Rapids, and Beijing National Symphony Orchestras to name a few, and has recorded on Gasparo and Centaur record labels with her husband, concert clarinetist Arthur Campbell. They have had numerous collaborative performances broadcast regionally, nationally, and internationally, on radio, television, and the Internet.

She performs and gives workshops throughout the country and at all of the national music teachers' conventions. She is the Director of Keyboard Publications for the FJH Music Company. Her articles can be read in *Keyboard Companion, The American Music Teacher,* and *Clavier* magazines. Her more than 60 educational piano CD's are recorded on Stargrass® Records. Dr. Marlais is an Associate Professor of Music at Grand Valley State University in Grand Rapids, Michigan, where she teaches piano majors, directs the piano pedagogy program, and coordinates all of the group piano programs, which includes the young beginner piano program. She received her DM in piano performance and pedagogy from Northwestern University and her MFA in piano performance from Carnegie Mellon University. She was named an Outstanding Alumnae by the University of Toledo, where she completed a BM in piano performance. She has also held full-time faculty piano positions at the Crane School of Music, S.U.N.Y. at Potsdam, Iowa State University, and Gustavus Adolphus College. Visit: www.helenmarlais.com.

Peggy O'Dell has been a piano teacher for over 25 years, having taught students in her private music studio as well as classes at Diablo Valley College in Pleasant Hill, California. She received a Bachelor of Music Education degree from the University of Kansas and holds a master's degree in music theory and composition from California State University in Hayward, California. Her piano instructors have included Hazel Troeger, a student of concert pianist Myra Hess, and Alexander Lieberman, a student of Egon Petri.

After teaching piano for over 15 years, she decided to pursue postgraduate studies in film scoring at the University of Southern California. While a student there, she received an award from BMI for the most outstanding student film score, which was written for full orchestra. She was also a guest lecturer at UCLA on the subject of piano pedagogy. She is an active member and past president of the Contra Costa County branch of the Music Teachers' Association of California. As a member of this association, she entered the state composition contest for teachers, won first place, and her winning two-piano work was performed at the annual state convention. Peggy currently resides in Alamo, California, where she continues to teach piano to students of all ages and abilities.

Kristen Avila runs an active piano studio, and especially enjoys teaching her students through games and activities. She has received piano pedagogy certificates from Indiana-Purdue University in Fort Wayne, Indiana, and from Grand Valley State University in Grand Rapids, Michigan. She is active in her local chapter of GMMTA, and has recently earned MMTA certification for the state of Michigan. She studies piano with Dr. Helen Marlais, and has been a member of Sigma Alpha Iota and Phi Kappa Phi. Kristen lives in Muskegon, Michigan, with her husband, Jim, and their six children. She enjoys scrapbooking, cross-stitching, camping, and playing cards (especially euchre).

TABLE OF CONTENTS

UNIT 1

Learn Your Theory: Ledger Lines 4
Write and Play Your Theory 5
The Candy Counter 6
Count and Hear Your Theory 7
Write and Play Your Theory 8
Lesson Day 9

UNIT 2

Learn Your Theory: Intervals 10
Write and Play Your Theory 11
It's Laundry Time! 12
Count and Hear Your Theory 13
Write and Play Your Theory 14
Lesson Day 15

UNIT 3

Learn Your Theory: Sharps and Flats 16
Count and Hear Your Theory 17
Write and Play Your Theory 18
Lesson Day 19

UNIT 4

Learn Your Theory: Half Steps and Whole Steps . . 20
Learn Your Theory: Major and Minor
   Five-Finger Patterns 21
Write and Play Your Theory 22
Learn Your Theory: Note Values 23
Count and Hear Your Theory 23
Write and Play Your Theory 24
Balloons 25
Lesson Day 26

UNIT 5

Learn Your Theory: Major and Minor Triads 27
Write and Play Your Theory 28
Count and Hear Your Theory 29
Write and Play Your Theory 30
My Heart Is Full 31
Lesson Day 32

UNIT 6

Learn Your Theory: Major One-Octave Scales . . 33-35
Write Your Theory 36
Count and Hear Your Theory 37
Write Your Theory 38
Lesson Day 39

UNIT 7

Learn Your Theory: Major Key Signatures 40-41
Write Your Theory 42
Learn Your Theory: Time Signatures 43
Learn Your Theory: Note Values 43
Write Your Theory 44
Learn Your Theory: Stem Rules 44
Write and Play Your Theory 44
Lesson Day 45

UNIT 8

Learn Your Theory: Vocabulary 46-48
Write Your Theory 49
Count and Hear Your Theory 50
Write and Play Your Theory 51
Question Wheels 52
Lesson Day 53

UNIT 9

Music Analysis 54-56

UNIT 10

Final Test 57-62
Circle of Fifths 63
Certificate of Achievement 64

Ledger Lines

Ledger Lines — lines drawn above or below the staff.

Ledger line notes in the treble clef.

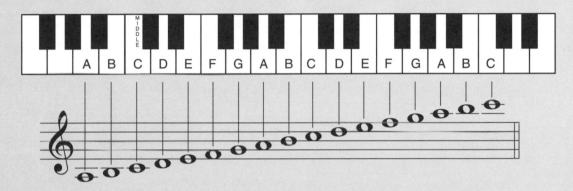

Find and play all of these notes.

Ledger line notes in the bass clef.

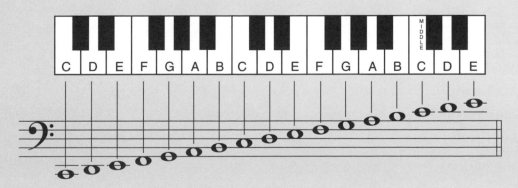

Find and play all of these notes.

Write and Play Your Theory

 Staff Notes

 Write the letter name of each note. The first one is done for you.
Then play each note.

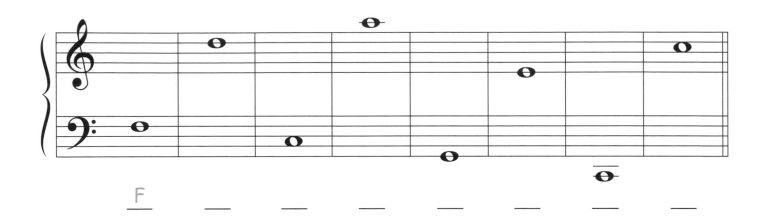

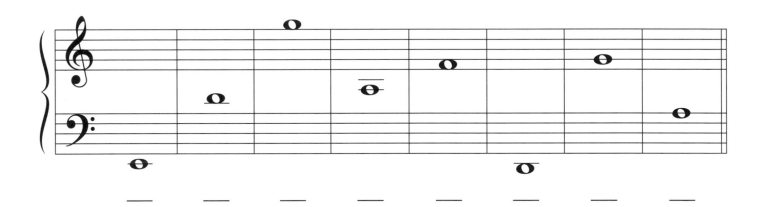

The Candy Counter

The pieces of candy below need to be sorted and counted. Looking at the color code box, color each candy the correct color, and then fill in the answers below.

Color Code	
letter	**color**
A	red
B	orange
C	yellow
D	green
E	blue

	red	orange	yellow	green	blue
5					
4					
3					
2					
1					

FJH2010

Count and Hear Your Theory

 Rhythm

 Write the note value under each note or rest. The first measure is done for you.

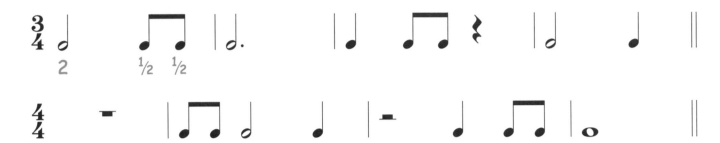

 Write in the name of these notes and rests.

𝐨 = _____

𝅗𝅥𝅘𝅥 = _____

𝄐 = _____

𝄽 = _____

𝅗𝅥. = _____

𝄾 = _____

 Ear Training

 Your teacher will play *one* of the melodies below.
Which one did you hear? Circle it.

Write and Play Your Theory

  Staff Notes

 What words do these notes spell? Write the answers and then play them.

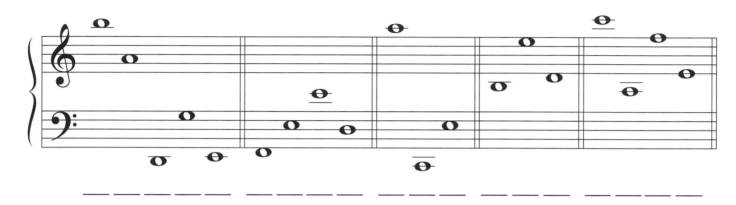

__ __ __   __ __ __ __   __ __ __   __ __ __   __ __ __

 Rhythm

 Draw these notes or rests:

dotted half note = _____   quarter rest = _____   two eighth notes = _____

whole rest = _____   half rest = _____   quarter note = _____

 Write the counting under the notes below. The first measure is done for you.
Then clap the rhythm, counting aloud.

$\frac{4}{4}$ ♩ ♫ ♩ 𝅗𝅥 | ♫♫ ♩ 𝄽 | 𝄼 ♩ ♫ ♩ ♫ ♩ 𝄽 ‖

1 + 2 + 3 + 4 +

FJH2010

Rhythm Clapback

Your teacher will clap *one* of the rhythms below.

Clap back the one you hear. Now, clap the other one.

Keyboard Playback

Your teacher will play *one* of the musical examples below.

Play back the one you hear. Now, play the other one.

Staff Notes

There are four measures of notes below. Your teacher will call out the measure number you are to play, in ANY order. Say the letter names as you play the notes. Use ONLY finger number 2.

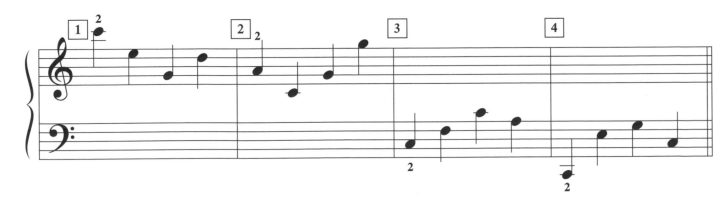

Learn Your Theory

Intervals

An interval is the distance between two notes on the staff or the keyboard, such as 2nd, 3rd, 4th, 5th, 6th, 7th, or 8th (octave).

2nd — no notes are skipped.

3rd — one note is skipped.

4th — two notes are skipped.

5th — three notes are skipped.

6th — four notes are skipped.

7th — five notes are skipped.

8th (octave) — six notes are skipped.

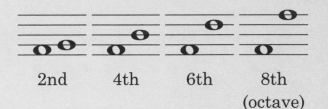

line to space or space to line

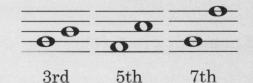

line to line or space to space

on the staff

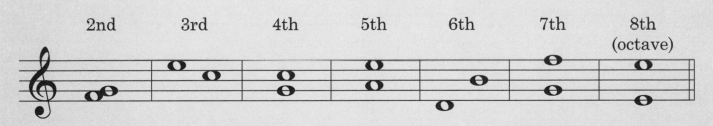

on the keyboard

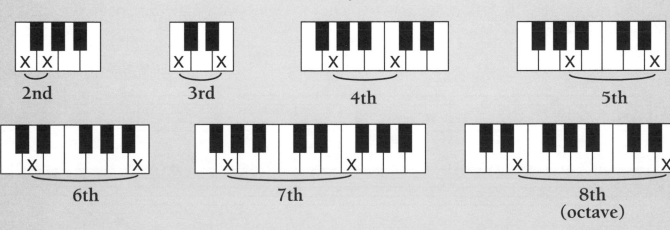

FJH2010

Write and Play Your Theory

  Intervals

Name each interval: 2nd, 3rd, 4th, 5th, 6th, 7th, or 8th (octave).
Then play them. The first one is done for you.

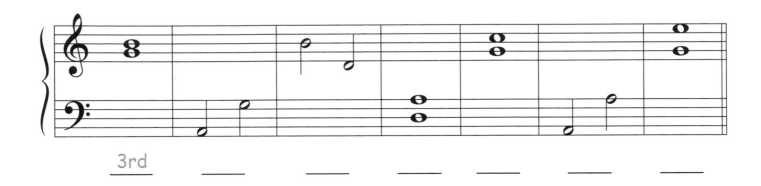

3rd

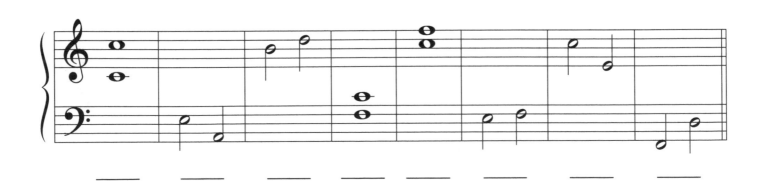

It's Laundry Time!

Today is laundry day, and everything is folded and put away — except for the socks! Help out by matching the correct intervals with a line. When you are done, color the socks so they match.

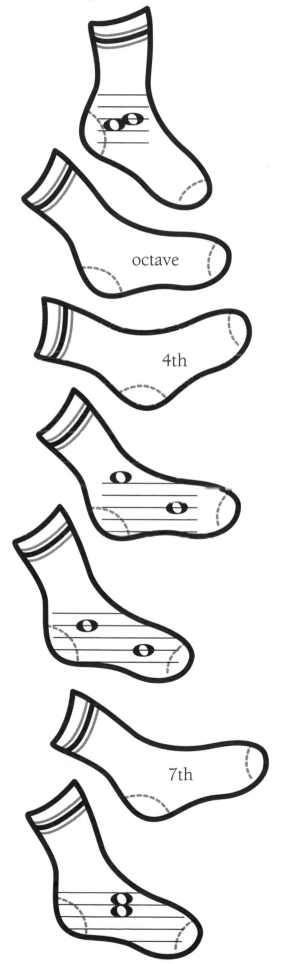

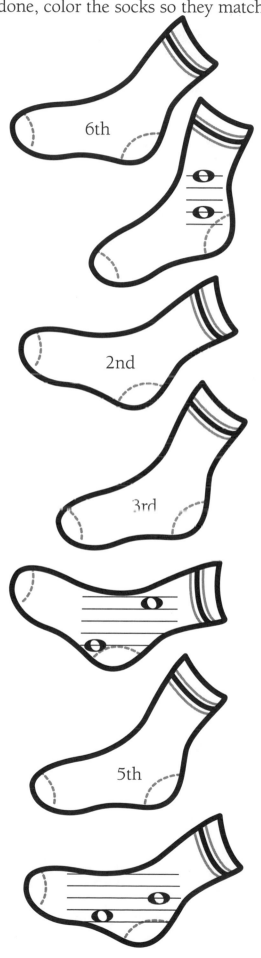

FJH2010

Count and Hear Your Theory

  Rhythm

 Match the notes or rests with the correct number of beats in $\frac{4}{4}$ time.

a. ▬ _____ 2 beats

b. 𝅗𝅥. _____ 4 beats

c. ♫ _____ 1 beat

d. ▬ _____ 3 beats

 Write the counting under the notes below. Then clap the rhythm, counting aloud.

 Ear Training

 Your teacher will play *one* of the intervals in each musical example below.
Circle the interval you hear.

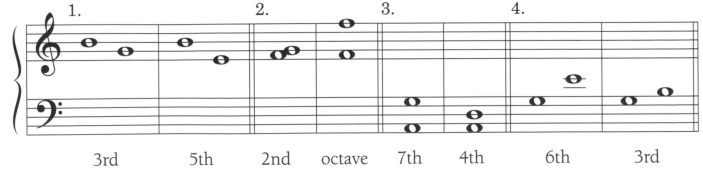

Write and Play Your Theory

 Staff Notes

 Draw the notes on the staff below. The first measure is done for you. Then play them.

two E's   three C's   two G's   three A's   three B's

 Intervals

 Draw intervals above or below the given note. Then play them.

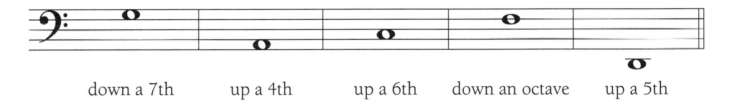

down a 7th   up a 4th   up a 6th   down an octave   up a 5th

 Rhythm

 Draw these notes or rests:

whole rest = _____   whole note = _____   quarter note = _____

half note = _____   half rest = _____   dotted half note = _____

quarter rest = _____   two eighth notes = _____

FJH2010

Rhythm Clapback

 Your teacher will clap *one* of the rhythms below.

Clap back the one you hear. Now, clap the other one.

Ear Training

 Your teacher will play *one* of the intervals in each musical example below.
Which one did you hear, A or B? Circle it.

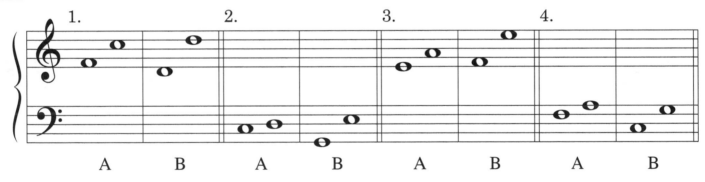

Staff Notes

There are four measures of notes below. Your teacher will call out the measure number
you are to play, in ANY order. Say the letter names as you play the notes. Use ONLY
finger number 2.

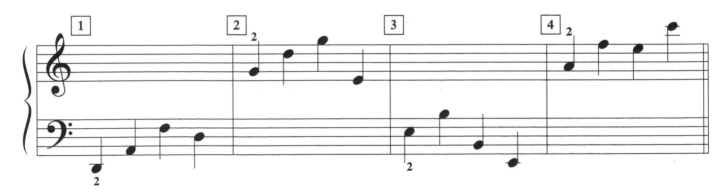

 **Learn Your Theory**

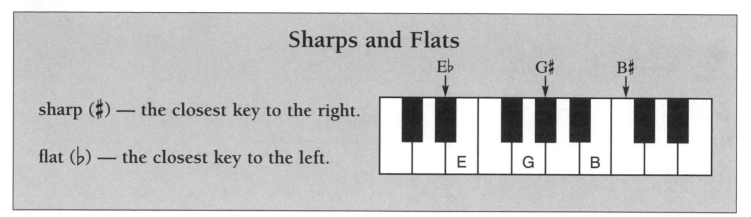

Sharps and Flats

sharp (♯) — the closest key to the right.

flat (♭) — the closest key to the left.

Give *two* names to the key that is checked. The first *two* are done for you.

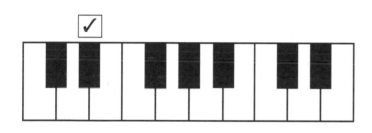

F♯   G♭

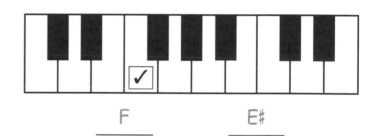

F   E♯

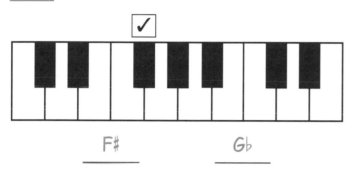

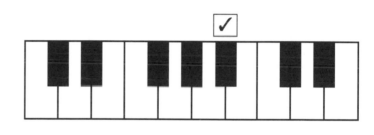

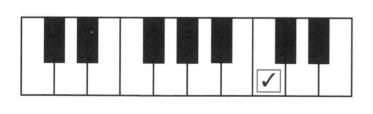

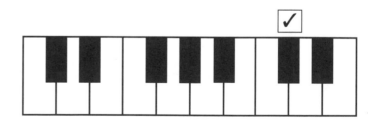

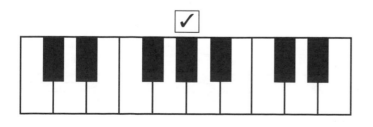

FJH2010

Count and Hear Your Theory

 Rhythm

 Write the counting under the notes. Then add the bar lines.

 Match each rest with the correct name.

a. ▬   _____ quarter rest

b. 𝄽   _____ half rest

c. ▬   _____ whole rest

 Ear Training

 Your teacher will play *one* of the intervals in each musical example below.
Circle the interval you hear.

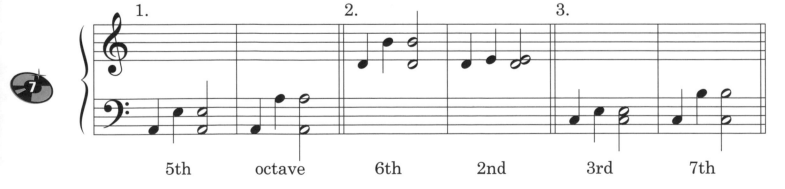

Write and Play Your Theory

 Sharps and Flats

 Draw *two* notes on the staff that match the key marked on the keyboard. The first one is done for you. Find and play the note on the piano.

    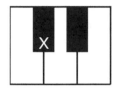 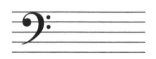

    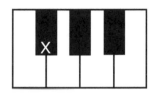 

 Intervals

 Draw a circle ○ around the 4th.

Draw a rectangle ☐ around the 7th.

Draw a diamond ◇ around the 3rd.

Draw an oval ◯ around the octave.

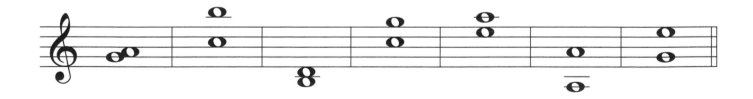

FJH2010

 Rhythm Clapback

 Your teacher will clap *one* of the rhythms below.

Clap back the one you hear. Now, clap the other one.

 Keyboard Playback

 Your teacher will play *one* of the musical examples below.

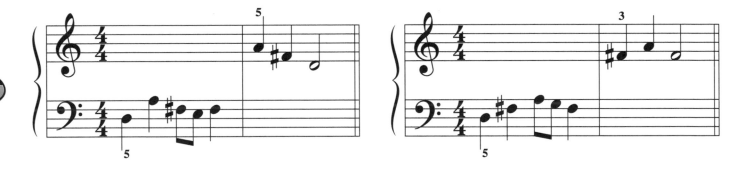

Play back the one you hear. Now, play the other one.

 Staff Notes

 There are four measures of notes below. Your teacher will call out the measure number you are to play, in ANY order. Say the letter names as you play the notes. Use ONLY finger number 2.

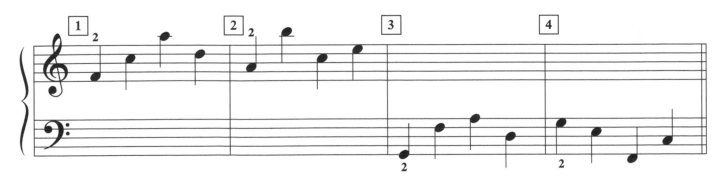

💡 **Learn Your Theory**

Half Steps and Whole Steps

Half step — from one key to the closest key.

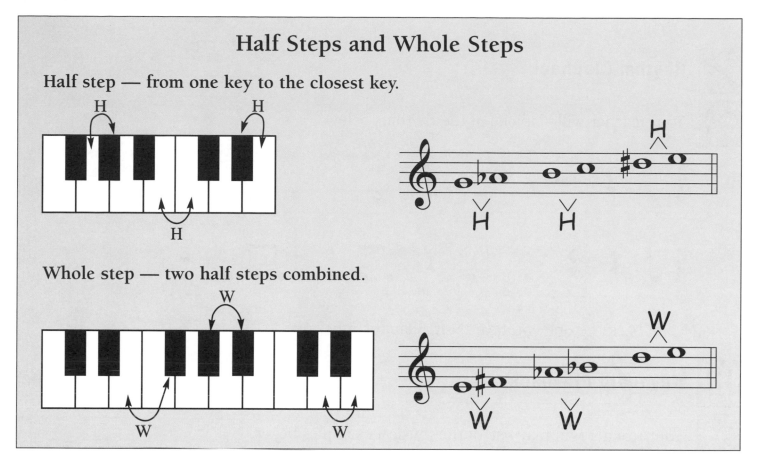

Whole step — two half steps combined.

🎹 **Half and Whole Steps**

✏️ Identify these half steps or whole steps. Write W for whole step and H for half step. Then play them on the piano.

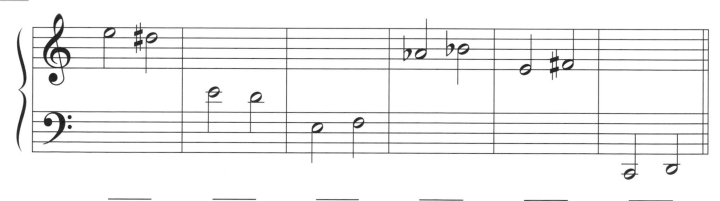

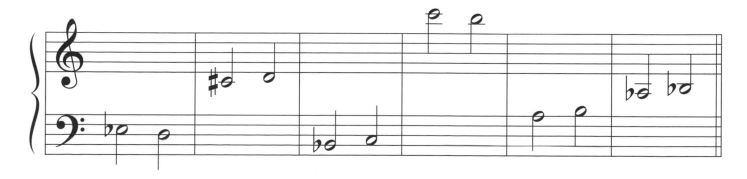

FJH2010

Major and Minor Five-Finger Patterns

A *Major* five-finger pattern is made up of all whole steps
except a half step between the *3rd* and *4th* keys.

D Major Five-Finger Pattern

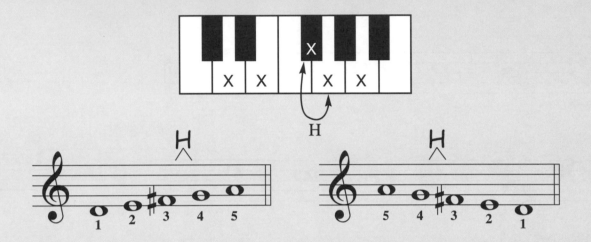

A *minor* five-finger pattern is made up of all whole steps
except a half step between the *2nd* and *3rd* keys.

d minor Five-Finger Pattern

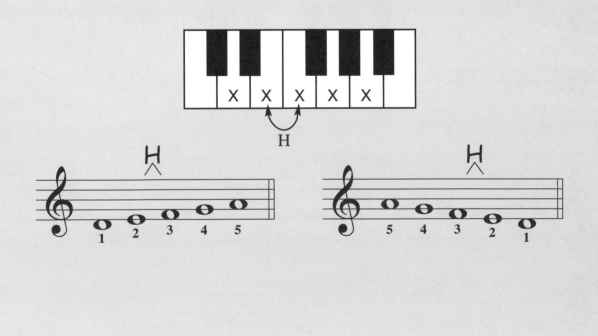

Write and Play Your Theory

 Major and Minor Five-Finger Patterns

 Name each five-finger pattern. Indicate if it is Major or minor.
Then play them. The first one is done for you.

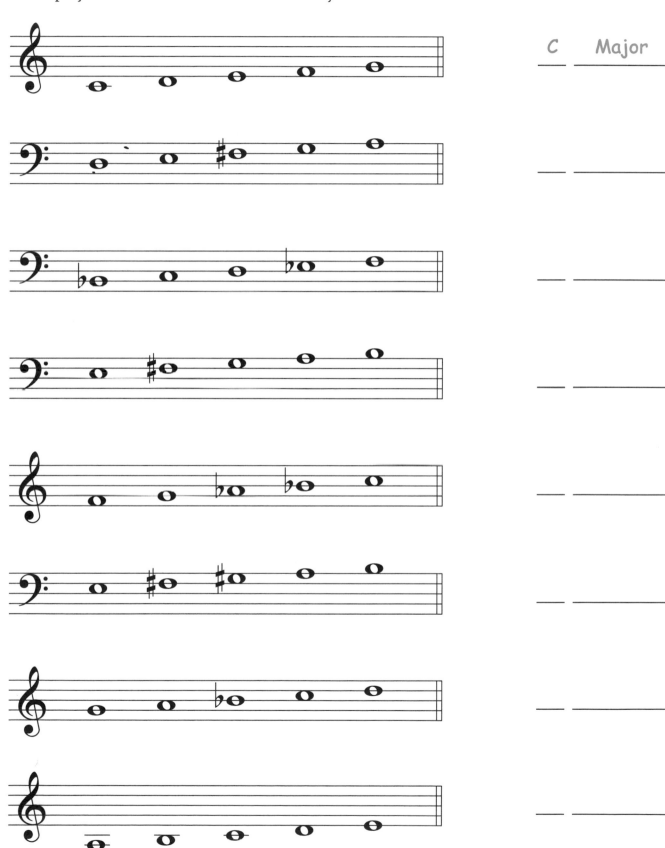

C   Major

Learn Your Theory

Note Values

♪ = eighth note = ½ beat   ↱ = eighth rest = ½ beat

Count and Hear Your Theory

 Rhythm

 Add the beats and give the total for the following time signatures.

$\frac{4}{4}$ ▬ + ♩ + 𝄽 + ♫ + ♪ + ↱ = ___ beats

$\frac{3}{4}$ ▬ + ♩ + ♩. + ↱ + ♪ + ▬ = ___ beats

 Draw one note to complete each measure.

 Ear Training

 Your teacher will play *both* of the pitches in each musical example below, in ANY order. Circle the pitch you hear *first,* A or B.

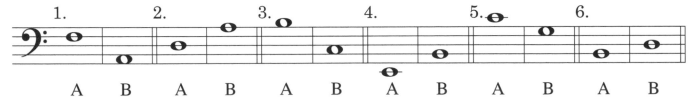

Your teacher will play *one* of the five-finger patterns in each musical example below. Which one did you hear, Major or minor? Circle it.

Write and Play Your Theory

  Half and Whole Steps

 Identify these whole or half steps. Write W for whole step and H for half step.
Then play them on the piano.

 Major and Minor Five-Finger Patterns

 Name each five-finger pattern. Indicate if it is Major or minor. Then play them.
Example: F Major

Intervals

 Draw an interval above or below the given note.

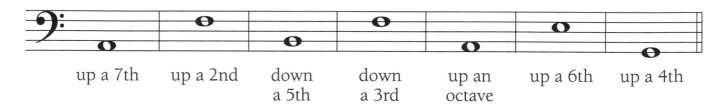

| up a 7th | up a 2nd | down
a 5th | down
a 3rd | up an
octave | up a 6th | up a 4th |

FJH2010

Balloons

The balloons below are missing their strings and need to be tied to the correct weight so they don't fly away. Draw a string from each balloon to the correct weight — Major or minor.

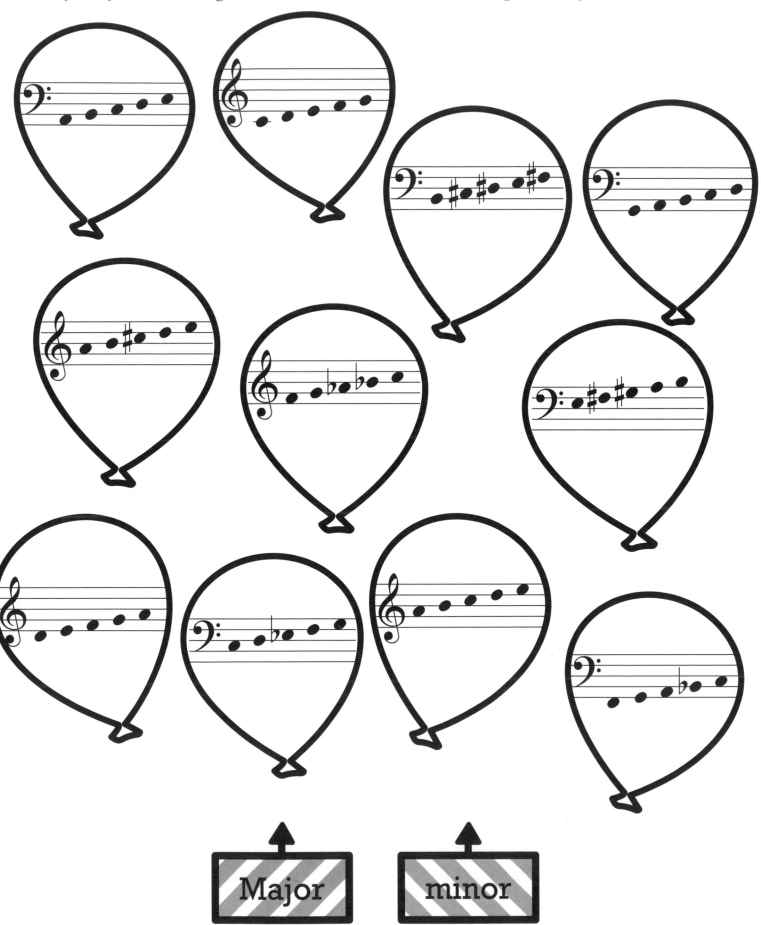

  Rhythm Clapback

 Your teacher will clap *one* of the rhythms below.

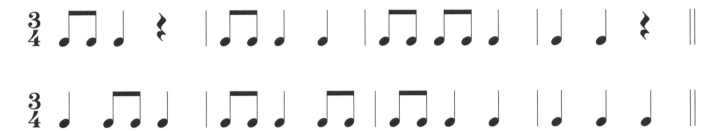

Clap back the one you hear. Now, clap the other one.

  Ear Training

 Your teacher will play *one* of the five-finger patterns in each musical example below. Which one did you hear, Major or minor? Circle it.

  Staff Notes

There are four measures of notes below. Your teacher will call out the measure number you are to play, in ANY order. Say the letter names as you play the notes. Use ONLY finger number 2.

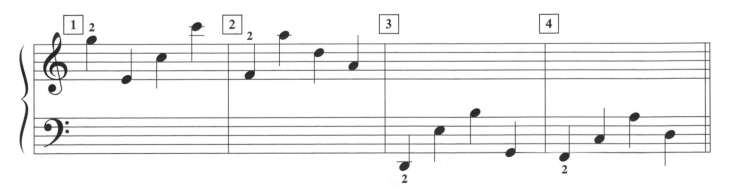

26   FJH2010

 **Learn Your Theory**

Major and Minor Triads

A *Major triad* is made up of the 1st, 3rd, and 5th notes
of a Major five-finger pattern.

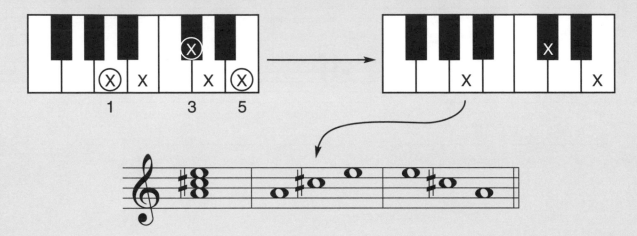

A *minor triad* is made up of the 1st, 3rd, and 5th notes
of a minor five-finger pattern.

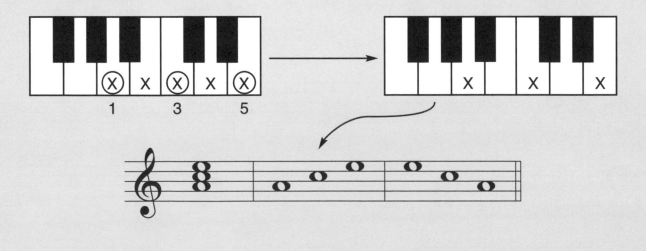

Write and Play Your Theory

 Major and Minor Triads

 Name each triad. Indicate if it is Major or minor.
Then play them. The first one is done for you.

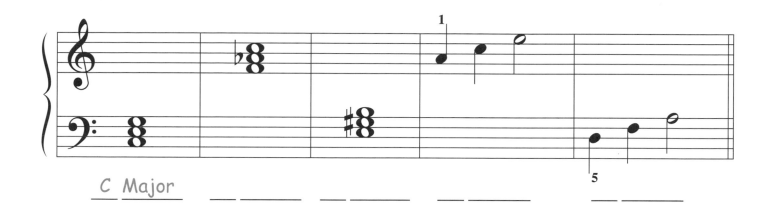

C Major ___ ___ ___ ___

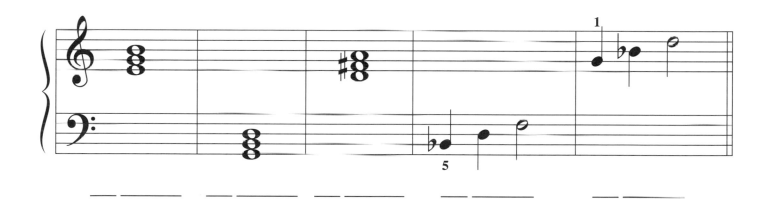

___ ___ ___ ___ ___

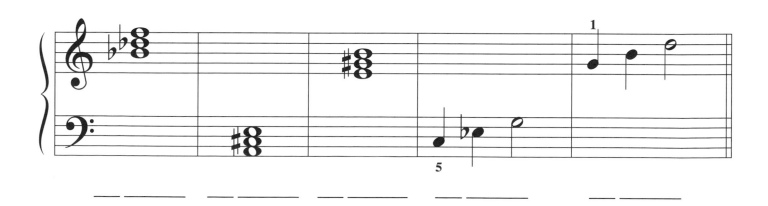

___ ___ ___ ___

FJH2010

Count and Hear Your Theory

 Rhythm

 Match each note with the correct name.

a. 𝅗𝅥.   ___ two eighth notes

b. ♪   ___ half note

c. ♩   ___ quarter note

d. 𝅗𝅥   ___ eighth note

e. ♫   ___ dotted half note

 Write the counting under the notes and add the bar lines. Then clap and count aloud.

 Ear Training

 Your teacher will play *one* of the triads in each musical example below.
Which one did you hear, Major or minor? Circle it.

 Your teacher will play *one* of the melodies in each musical example below.
Which one did you hear, A or B? Circle it.

Write and Play Your Theory

Staff Notes

Draw the following:

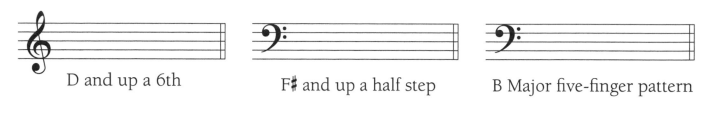

D and up a 6th   F♯ and up a half step   B Major five-finger pattern

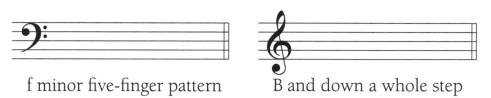

f minor five-finger pattern   B and down a whole step

Triads

Name each triad. Indicate if it is Major or minor. Then play them.

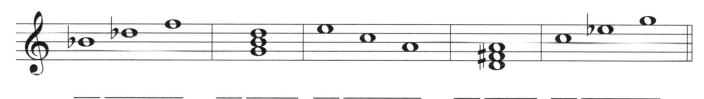

— — —   — — —   — — —   — — —

Staff Notes

Write the notes that spell these words. The first one is done for you.

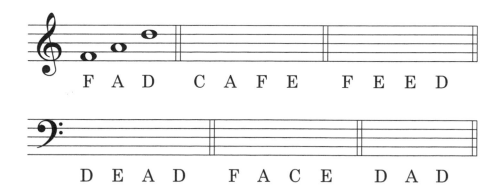

F A D   C A F E   F E E D

D E A D   F A C E   D A D

My Heart Is Full

Complete each heart by filling in the empty half with the correct answer (M for Major triad or m for minor triad). When you are done, color the Major-triad hearts red and the minor-triad hearts pink. Play the triads on the piano.

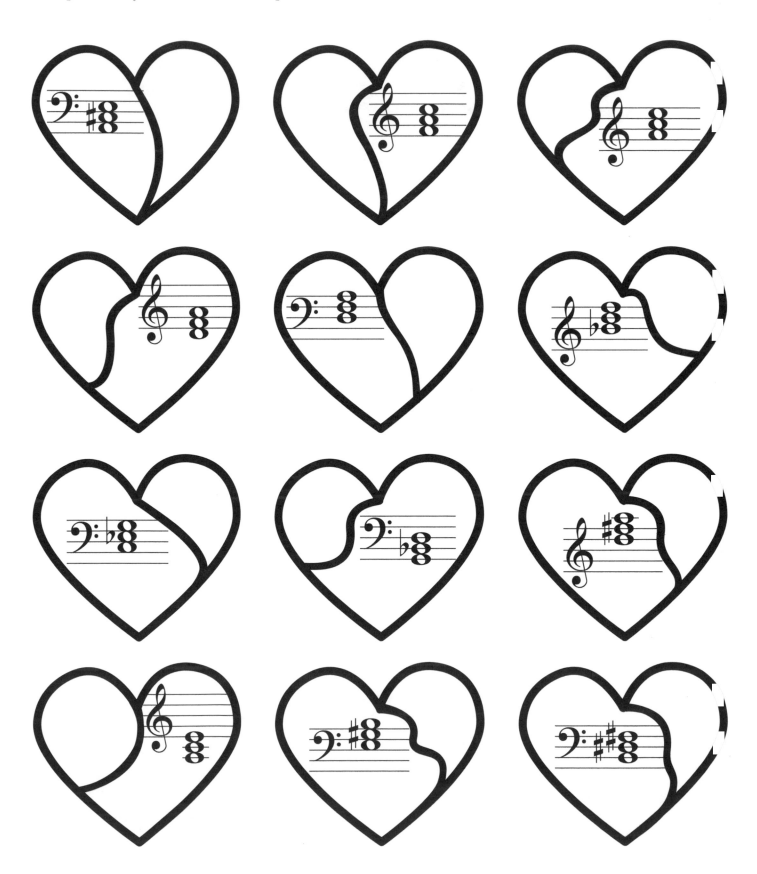

Rhythm Clapback

16

Your teacher will clap *one* of the rhythms below.

Clap back the one you hear. Now, clap the other one.

Ear Training

17

Your teacher will play *one* of the triads in each musical example below. Which one did you hear, Major or minor? Circle it.

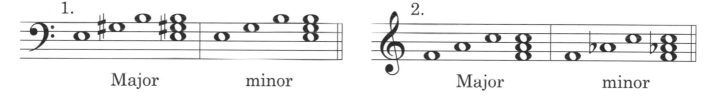

Staff Notes

There are four measures of notes below. Your teacher will call out the measure number you are to play, in ANY order. Say the letter names as you play the notes. Use ONLY finger number 2.

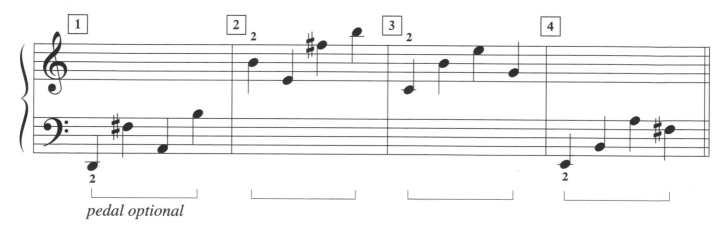

pedal optional

FJH2010

Major One-Octave Scales

There are two methods for determining what sharps or flats belong to a Major scale.

Method #1:

Major scales consist of all whole steps, except there are *half steps* between the 3rd and 4th, and 7th and 8th steps (degrees) of the scale.

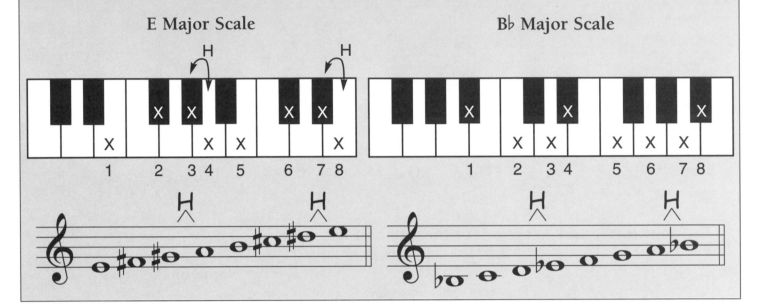

Major One-Octave Scales

 On the keyboard below, mark the keys that belong to the A Major scale. Indicate the half steps with an H.

 Now, on the staff below, draw the sharps that belong to the A Major scale. Indicate the half steps with an H.

A Major

Major One-Octave Scales

Method #2:

Scales with sharps

1. Use the first letter from each word in this sentence:

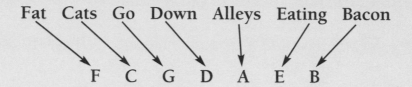

Fat   Cats   Go   Down   Alleys   Eating   Bacon

F   C   G   D   A   E   B

2. Find the name of the scale. In this example, we will use E Major.

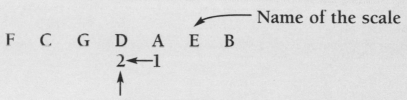

← Name of the scale

F   C   G   D   A   E   B

3. Count *two letters to the left* of the name of the scale.

← Name of the scale

F   C   G   D   A   E   B
　　　　2←1
　　　　　↑
Two letters to the left of the scale name

4. The *letter you land on plus all the letters to the left of it are the sharps* that belong to the scale.

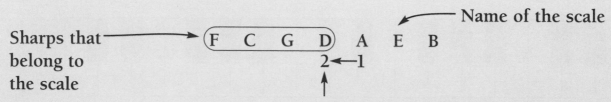

← Name of the scale

Sharps that belong to the scale ──→ (F   C   G   D)   A   E   B
　　　　　　　　　　　　　　　　2←1
　　　　　　　　　　　　　　　　 ↑
Two letters to the left of the scale name

5. The sharps that belong to the E Major scale are F♯, C♯, G♯, and D♯.

34

FJH2010

Scales with flats

1. Use the first letter of each word in this sentence:

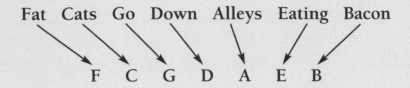

Fat   Cats   Go   Down   Alleys   Eating   Bacon

F   C   G   D   A   E   B

2. Then put the letters in *reverse* order.

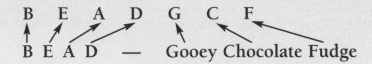

B   E   A   D   G   C   F

B E A D   —   Gooey Chocolate Fudge

3. Find the name of the scale. In this example, we will use B♭ Major.

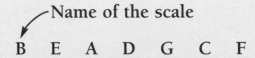

Name of the scale

B   E   A   D   G   C   F

4. Count *one letter to the right* of the name of the scale.

Name of the scale

B   E   A   D   G   C   F
→1

One letter to the right of the scale name

5. The *letter you land on plus all the letters to the left of it are the flats* that belong to the scale.

Name of the scale

Flats that belong to the scale → (B   E)   A   D   G   C   F
→1

One letter to the right of the scale name

6. The flats that belong to the B♭ Major scale are B♭ and E♭.

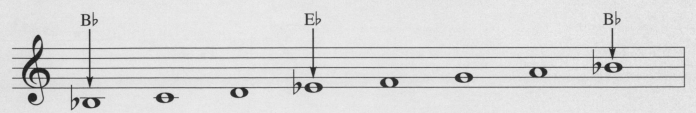

7. The key of F having one flat – B♭ – must be memorized.

Write Your Theory

Major One-Octave Scales

Add the sharps (♯) or flats (♭) to form these Major scales.
Mark the half steps. The first one is done for you.

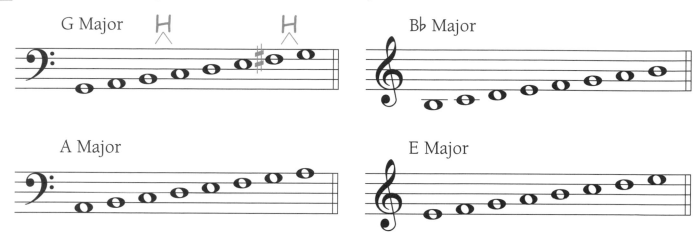

G Major

Bb Major

A Major

E Major

Circle the sharps or flats that belong to the following Major scales. Then add
the sharps (♯) or flats (♭) to the scales on the right. The first one is done for you.

Sharp scales — *two* letters to the *left*

D Major

(F C) G D A E B

A Major

F C G D A E B

E Major

F C G D A E B

Flat scales — *one* letter to the *right*

Bb Major

B E A D G C F

*F Major

B E A D G C F

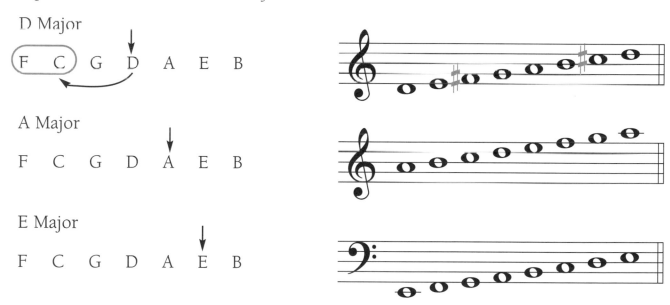

* If you prefer, just memorize that the scale of F Major has a B flat.

FJH2010

Count and Hear Your Theory

 Rhythm

 Put a check (✔) by the correct time signature.

 Ear Training

 Your teacher will play *one* of the scales below.
The first scale is played with a crescendo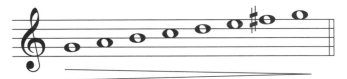
The second scale is played with a decrescendo, also called a diminuendo ⟩ .
Circle the one your hear.

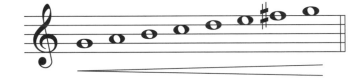 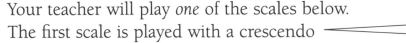

 Your teacher will play *one* of the rhythms below. Circle the one your hear.

Write Your Theory

Scales

 On the keyboards below, mark the keys that belong to the given scales.
The first one is done for you.

G Major

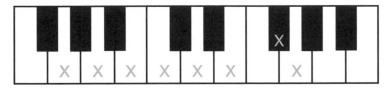

A Major

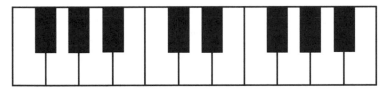

F Major

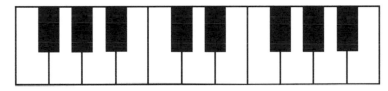

D Major

 Circle the sharps or flats that belong to the following Major scales.
Then add the sharps (♯) or flats (♭) to the scales on the right.

E Major

F   C   G   D   A   E   B

B♭ Major

B   E   A   D   G   C   F

A Major

F   C   G   D   A   E   B

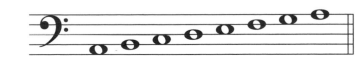

FJH2010

Rhythm Clapback

Your teacher will clap *one* of the rhythms below.

Clap back the one you hear. Now, clap the other one.

Keyboard Playback

Your teacher will play *one* of the musical examples below.

Play back the one you hear. Now, play the other one.

Staff Notes

There are four measures of notes below. Your teacher will call out the measure number you are to play, in ANY order. Say the letter names as you play the notes. Use ONLY finger number 2.

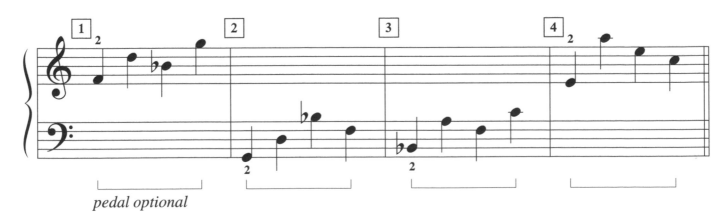

pedal optional

💡 **Learn Your Theory**

Major Key Signatures

Naming keys with sharps in the key signature.

Look at the last sharp (farthest away
from the clef sign) in a key signature.
Below, the circled ♯ is C♯.

C♯ is the 7th step of the
D Major scale.

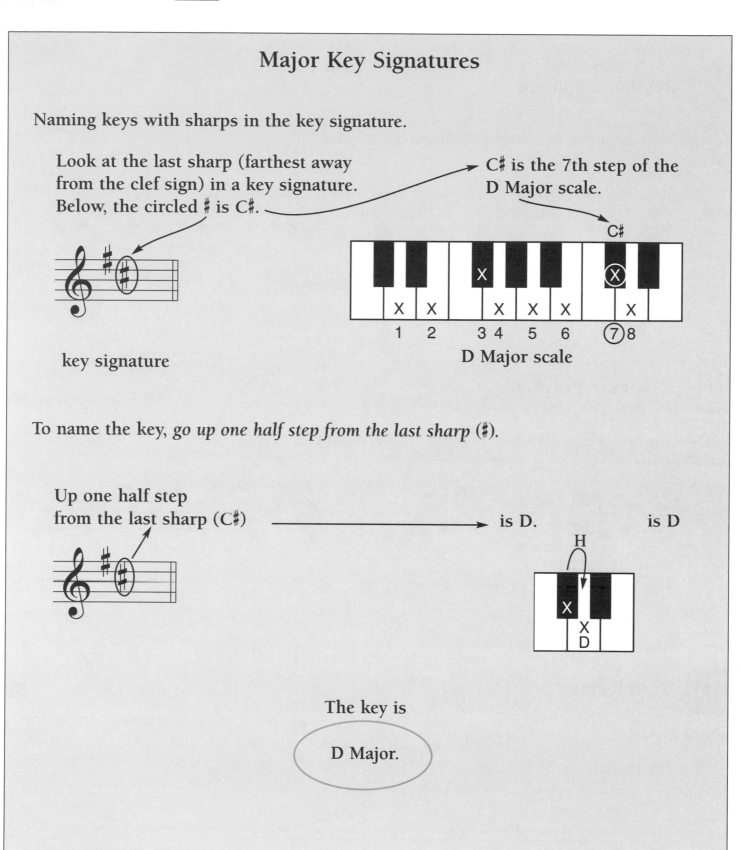

key signature

D Major scale

To name the key, *go up one half step from the last sharp (♯).*

Up one half step
from the last sharp (C♯)   is D.   is D

The key is

D Major.

FJH2010

Naming keys with flats in the key signature.

Look at the last flat in a key signature. Below, the circled ♭ is E♭.

E♭ is the 4th step of the Major scale.

key signature

B♭ Major scale

To name the key, *go down one half step and two whole steps from the last flat* (♭).

Down one half step and two whole steps from the last flat (♭)

is B♭.

The key is

B♭ Major.

Super shortcut:

When there are *two or more flats* in the key signature, it is quicker *to find the next to last flat,* which is the name of the key.

The next to last flat is B♭.

The key is

B♭ Major.

Write Your Theory

Major Key Signatures

 Circle the correct answers below.

In a key signature with sharps, the last sharp in the key signature is the **7th** **4th** step of the scale.

To name a key signature with sharps in it, go up one **half** **whole** step from the last sharp in the key signature.

In a key signature with flats, the last flat in the key signature is the **7th** **4th** step of the scale.

To name a key signature with flats in it, go down one **half** **whole** step and two **half** **whole** steps from the last flat in the key signature.

If there are two or more flats in a key signature, a quick way to find the answer is to use the **last** **next to last** flat in the key signature.

 Name the key signatures below. The first one is done for you.

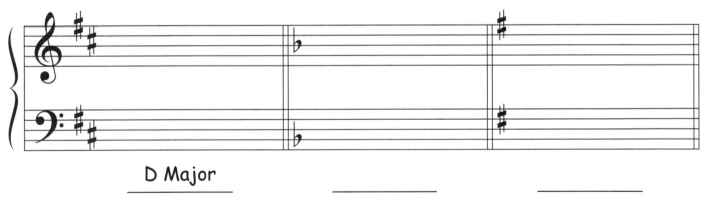

D Major _____   _____   _____

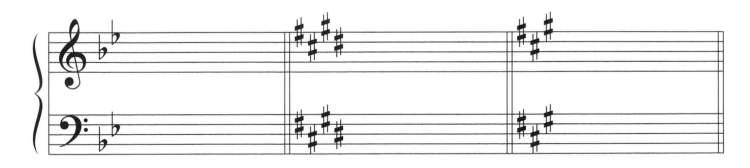

_____   _____   _____

FJH2010

Learn Your Theory

Time Signatures

$\mathbf{C}$ = common time = $\dfrac{4}{4}$

$\dfrac{2}{4}$ = 2 beats in each measure.
= a quarter note ($\quarternote$) gets 1 beat.

on the staff

Learn Your Theory

Note Values

New note:

$\dottedquarternote$ = dotted quarter note = 1½ beats

Rhythm

Draw *two rests* to complete each measure below.

Mark the note value under each note or rest. The first measure is done for you.

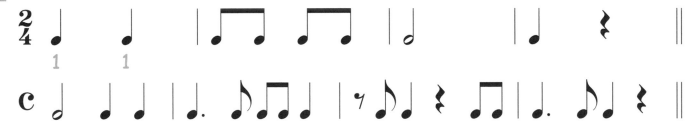

Ear Training

Your teacher will play *one* of the melodies below.
Which melody did you hear, Major or minor? Circle it.

minor   Major

Your teacher will play *one* of the rhythms below.
Which one did you hear? Circle it.

Write Your Theory

Key Signatures

 Name the key signatures below.

_____   _____   _____

_____   _____   _____

💡 Learn Your Theory

Stem Rules

Notes on the *lower* half of the staff have stems that go *up* on the right side.

Notes on the *upper* half of the staff have stems that go *down* on the left side.

Notes on the middle line of the staff can go either up or down.

Write and Play Your Theory

 Staff Notes

 Draw the following staff notes and then play them.

Using a half note,
draw a D *high*
on the staff.

Using a quarter
note, draw a G
low on the staff.

Using an eighth
note, draw a B.

FJH2010

Rhythm Clapback

Your teacher will clap *one* of the rhythms below.

Clap back the one you hear. Now, clap the other one.

Keyboard Playback

Your teacher will play *one* of the musical examples below.

 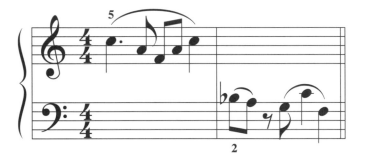

Play back the one you hear. Now, play the other one.

Staff Notes

There are four measures of notes below. Your teacher will call out the measure number you are to play, in ANY order. Say the letter names as you play the notes. Use ONLY finger number 2.

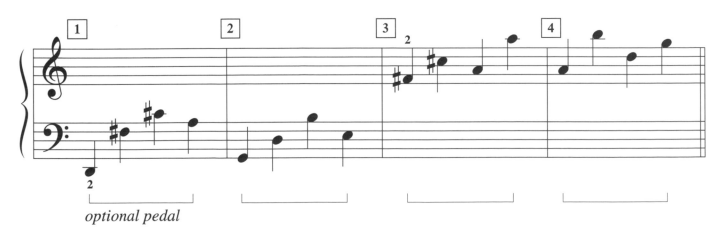

optional pedal

 **Learn Your Theory**

Vocabulary

a tempo		return to the original tempo
accidental*		a sharp or flat or natural placed before a note
common time	**C**	same as $\frac{4}{4}$
clefs:		
treble clef		play the notes above middle C
bass clef		play the notes below middle C
damper pedal*		the pedal on the far right; depress and release the damper pedal
D.C. al fine *da capo al fine*		return to the beginning and play to *fine*

dynamics: the signs that indicate how loud or soft to play

forte	*f*	loud
*fortissimo**	*ff*	very loud
mezzo forte	*mf*	moderately loud
piano	*p*	soft
*pianissimo**	*pp*	very soft

* These words are new to this book.

FJH2010

mezzo piano	**mp**	moderately soft
crescendo	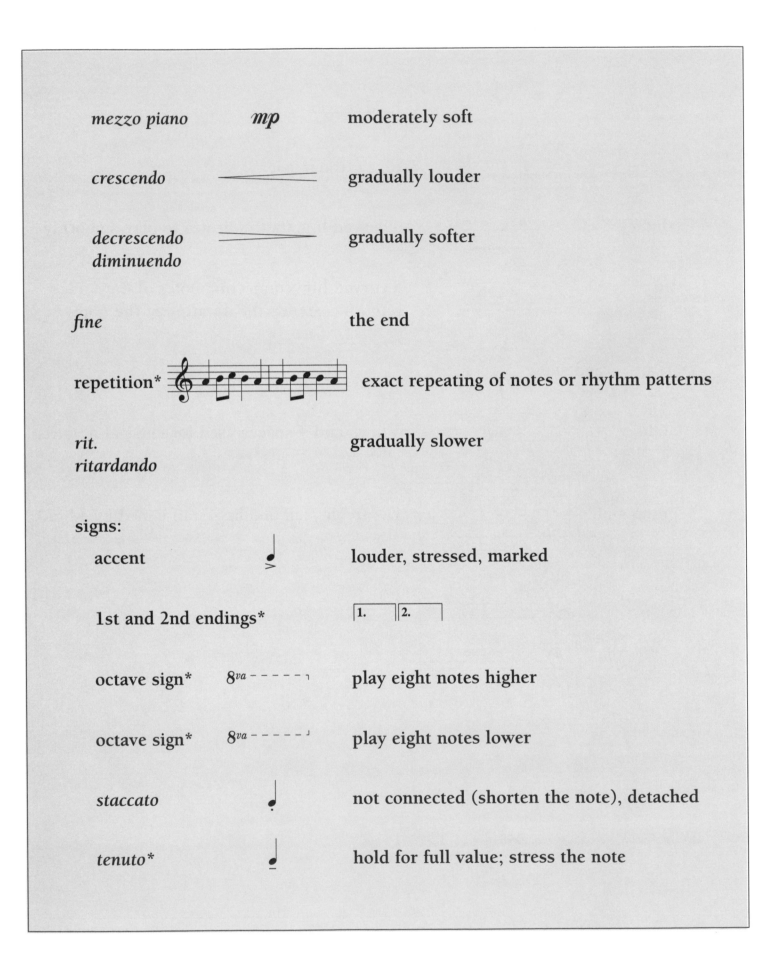	gradually louder
decrescendo *diminuendo*		gradually softer
fine		the end
repetition*		exact repeating of notes or rhythm patterns
rit. *ritardando*		gradually slower

signs:

accent		louder, stressed, marked
1st and 2nd endings*	1. 2.	
octave sign*	8*va* – – – – –	play eight notes higher
octave sign*	8*va* – – – – –	play eight notes lower
staccato		not connected (shorten the note), detached
*tenuto**		hold for full value; stress the note

fermata	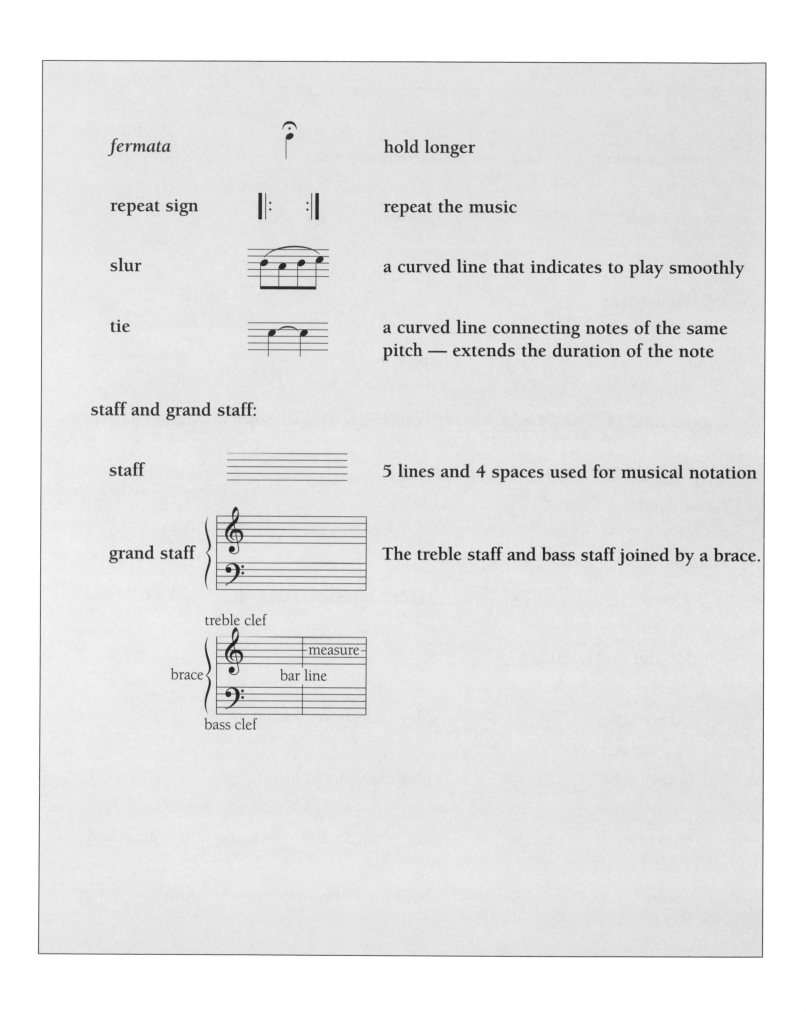	hold longer
repeat sign		repeat the music
slur		a curved line that indicates to play smoothly
tie		a curved line connecting notes of the same pitch — extends the duration of the note

staff and grand staff:

staff		5 lines and 4 spaces used for musical notation
grand staff		The treble staff and bass staff joined by a brace.

treble clef

brace

measure

bar line

bass clef

Write Your Theory

Signs and Terms

Match these items with the correct meaning or sign.

a. *fortissimo* _____   8*va* - - - - - ⌐

b. one octave lower _____ |1. |2.

c. one octave higher _____

d. *tenuto* _____

e. slur _____   **ff**

f. *pianissimo* _____

g. *fermata* _____   8*va* - - - - - ⌐

h. tie _____   very soft

i. 1st and 2nd endings _____

Match these items with the correct meaning or sign.

a. *crescendo* _____

b. repetition _____

c. accidentals _____   gradually louder

d. common time _____

e. *diminuendo* _____

f. treble clef _____

g. bass clef _____   **𝄢**

h. damper pedal _____   **C** same as $\frac{4}{4}$

Count and Hear Your Theory

Rhythm

 Write the counting under the notes and add the bar lines. Then clap and count aloud.

 Add the beats and give the total for the following time signatures.

$\frac{3}{4}$ ▬. + 𝄽 + ▬ + ♩. + ♪ + 𝅗𝅥. = ____ beats

$\frac{4}{4}$ ▬ + 𝄾 + ♪. + 𝅗𝅥 + ♫ + ▬ + ♩. + ♪ = ____ beats

Ear Training

 Your teacher will play *one* of the melodies below.
Which one did you hear? Circle it.

FJH2010

Write and Play Your Theory

 Staff Notes

 Using half notes, draw the following notes on the staff. Then play them.

3 C's 3 A's 2 F's

Key Signatures

 Name the Major key signatures below.

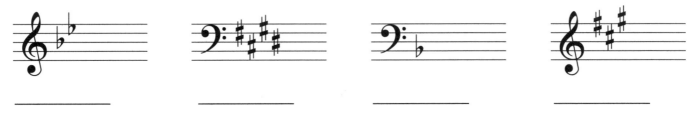

_____ _____ _____ _____

 Draw the following.

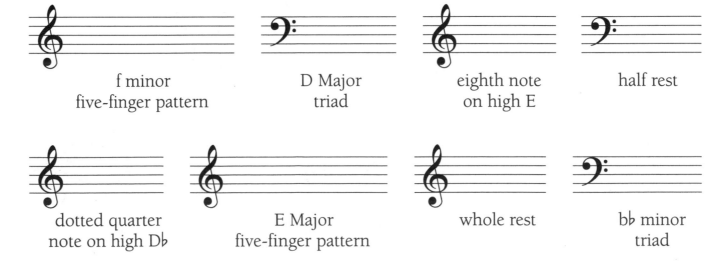

f minor
five-finger pattern

D Major
triad

eighth note
on high E

half rest

dotted quarter
note on high D♭

E Major
five-finger pattern

whole rest

b♭ minor
triad

Question Wheels

Using the words or symbols in the answer box, fill in the blanks in the question wheels that best fit the description.

Answer Box

crescendo
diminuendo
fermata
first & second endings
fortissimo
8va¬
8va⌐
pianissimo
primary triads
ritardando
repetition
slur

Rhythm Clapback

Your teacher will clap *one* of the rhythms below.

Clap back the one you hear. Now, clap the other one.

Keyboard Playback

Your teacher will play *one* of the musical examples below.

Play back the one you hear. Now, play the other one.

Staff Notes

There are four measures of notes below. Your teacher will call out the measure number you are to play, in ANY order. Say the letter names as you play the notes. Use ONLY finger number 2.

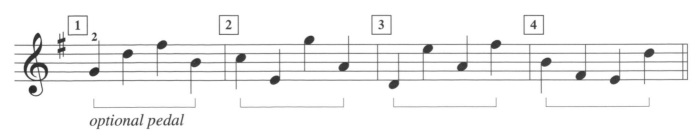

optional pedal

Music Analysis

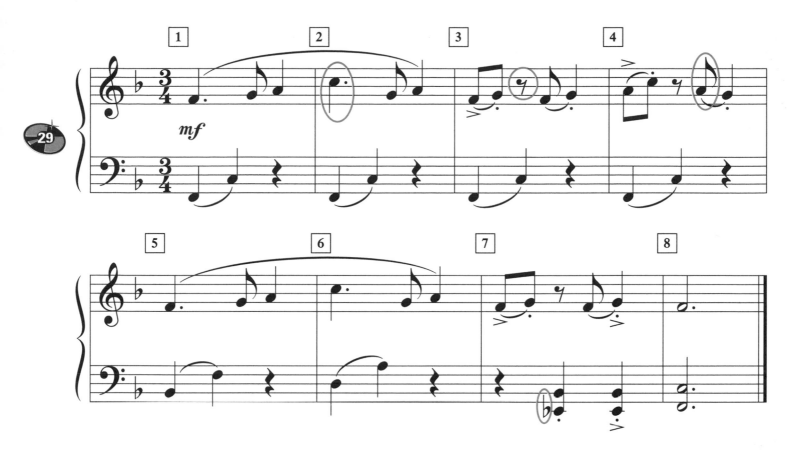

 Listen to track 29.

 Answer these questions about the music above. Circle the correct answer.

1. Name the key signature.	F Major	G Major
2. What is the meaning of the time signature?	play all B's flat	3 beats per measure
3. The circled note in measure 2 gets how many beats?	3	1½
4. The circled rest in measure 3 gets how many beats?	1	½
5. The circled note in measure 4 gets how many beats?	½	1
6. The left hand has the same interval in the entire piece. What is the name of this interval?	5th	4th
7. Which three measures have accents, slurs, and staccato?	3, 5, and 6	3, 4, and 7
8. Another name for the circled E♭ in measure 7 is?	natural	accidental

FJH2010

Music Analysis

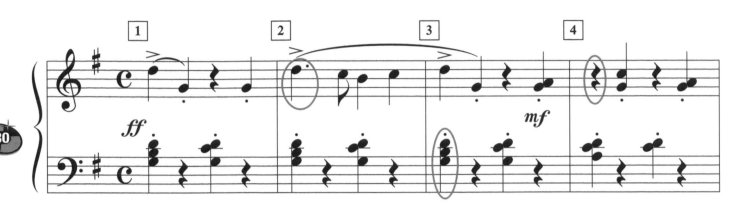

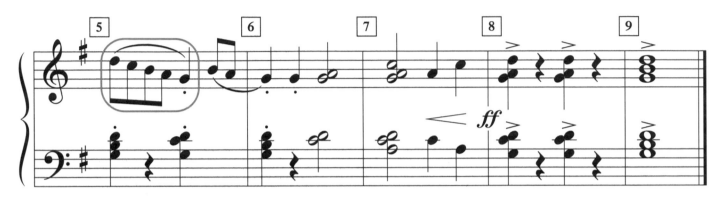

 Listen to track 30.

 Answer these questions about the music above. Circle the correct answer.

1. Name the key signature. | G Major | F Major

2. What does the **ff** in measure 1 mean? | very loud | very soft

3. What is the meaning of this symbol, **C**, which is found in the first measure? | **4/4** | **3/4**

4. What is the name of the five-finger pattern that is circled in measure 5? | D Major | G Major

5. What is the meaning of the dot after the note that is circled in measure 2? | detached | ½ beat

6. What is the name of the curved line in measure 1? | tie | slur

7. What is the name of the rest that is circled in measure 4? | eighth rest | quarter rest

Music Analysis

 Listen to track 31.

 Answer these questions about the music above. Circle the correct answer.

1. What does the **pp** in measure 1 mean?　　　　　very loud　　　　　very soft

2. Are the curved lines in the left hand in measures 1 and 2 ties or slurs?　　　　　ties　　　　　slurs

3. What is the name of the circled interval in measure 5?　　　　　6th　　　　　7th

4. What is the meaning of ⌐‿⌐ throughout the composition?　　　　　damper pedal　　　　　soft pedal

5. What is the name of the circled note in measure 3?　　　　　F♯　　　　　F

6. What is the meaning of *rit.* in measure 6?　　　　　gradually slower　　　　　gradually softer

7. What is the meaning of ⌢• in measure 7?　　　　　detached　　　　　hold longer

8. What is the meaning of ⟩ in measure 6?　　　　　gradually softer　　　　　gradually louder

FJH2010

UNIT 10   Final Test

 Name these notes on the staff. Then play them.

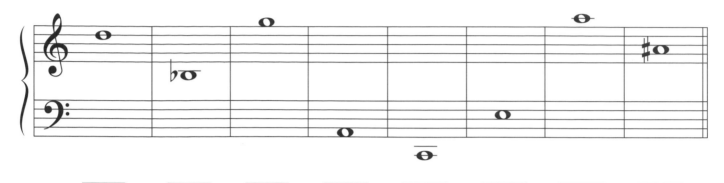

 Name these intervals. Then play them.

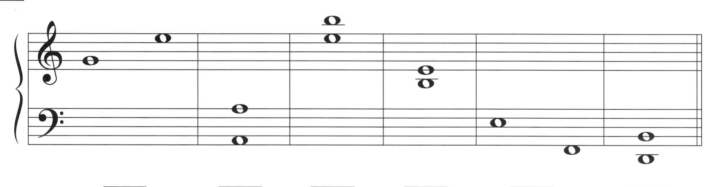

 Name these Major or minor five-finger patterns. Then play them.

Name these Major or minor triads. Then play them.

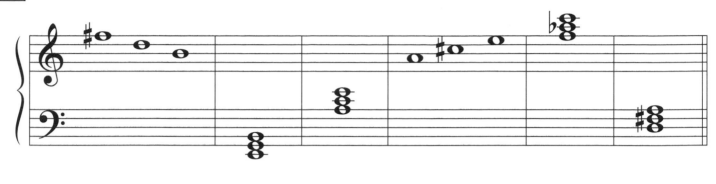

_____   _____   _____   _____   _____   _____

Add the note values and give the total number of beats for the following time signatures.

$\frac{4}{4}$ 𝅗𝅥. + 𝅝 + 𝅘𝅥𝅘𝅥 + 𝄾 + 𝅘𝅥𝅮 + 𝅏 + 𝄻 = ___ beats

$\frac{3}{4}$ 𝅗𝅥. + 𝅘𝅥𝅮 + 𝅘𝅥 + 𝄻 + 𝄽 + 𝅗𝅥. + 𝅘𝅥𝅘𝅥 = ___ beats

Write the counting under the notes and rests. Then add the bar lines.

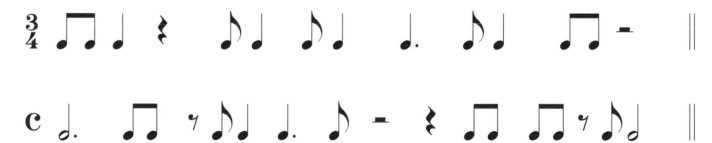

Answer the following questions.

The name of this note (𝅘𝅥𝅮) is _____ and it gets _____ beat(s).

The name of this note (𝅘𝅥.) is _____ and it gets _____ beat(s).

The name of this note (𝅗𝅥.) is _____ and it gets _____ beat(s).

The name of this rest (𝄻) is _____ and it gets _____ beat(s).

The name of this rest (𝄾) is _____ and it gets _____ beat(s).

The name of this rest (𝄽) is _____ and it gets _____ beat(s).

FJH2010

Name these Major key signatures.

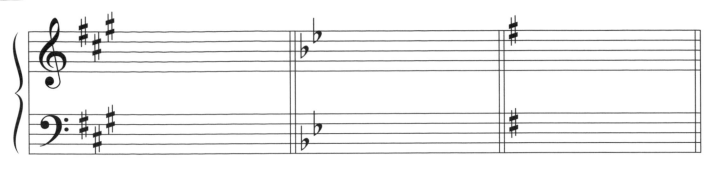

_____   _____   _____

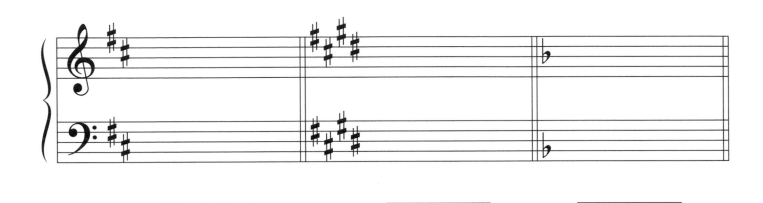

_____   _____   _____

 Add the sharps or flats to form these Major scales.

F Major   E Major

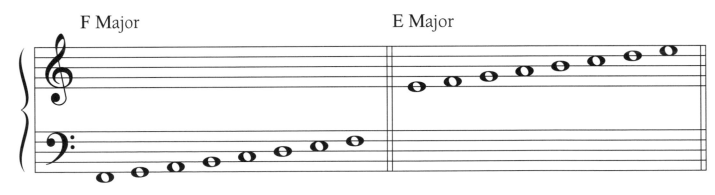

A Major   B♭ Major

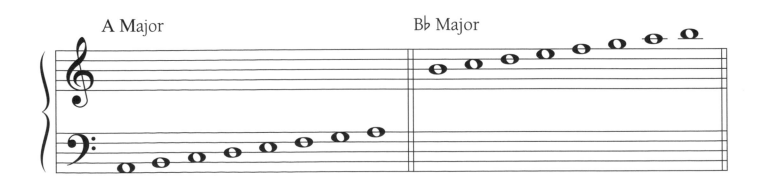

Match these items with the correct meaning or sign.

a. 1st and 2nd endings   _____ *pp*

b. *crescendo*   _____ *mf*

c. very loud   _____

d. accent   _____ *ff*

e. medium loud   _____

f. very soft   _____ gradually louder

g. *decrescendo*   _____

h. *tenuto*   _____

 Match these items with the correct meaning or sign.

a. dynamics   _____ *8va* – – – – – –

b. *ritardando*   _____

c. one octave higher   _____

d. one octave lower   _____ gradually slower

e. accidentals   _____ *8va* – – – – – –

f. treble clef   _____ how soft or loud to play

g. bass clef   _____

FJH2010

Your teacher will play or clap each musical example *two times*.

 Your teacher will clap *one* of the rhythms below.
Which one do you hear? Circle it.

 Your teacher will play *one* of the intervals in each musical example below.
Circle the one you hear, A or B.

 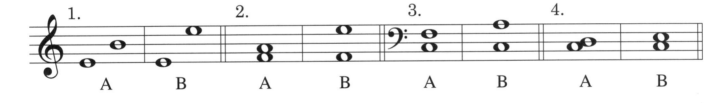

 Your teacher will play *one* of the melodies below.
Which one did you hear? Circle it.

 Listen to track 35.

 Answer these questions about the music above. Circle the correct answer.

1. No time signature is given. What should it be?	$\frac{3}{4}$	**c**
2. This piece is written in what key?	G Major	D Major
3. What is the name of the scale in measure 3?	G Major	D Major
4. The circled note in measure 1 gets how many beats?	1½	1
5. The dynamic marking in measure 7 is called?	crescendo	slur
6. The circled interval in measure 8 is called?	an octave	a 7th
7. What is the name of the five-finger pattern in the left hand in measure 3?	d minor	D Major
8. Name the rest that is circled in measure 2.	quarter rest	eighth rest

FJH2010

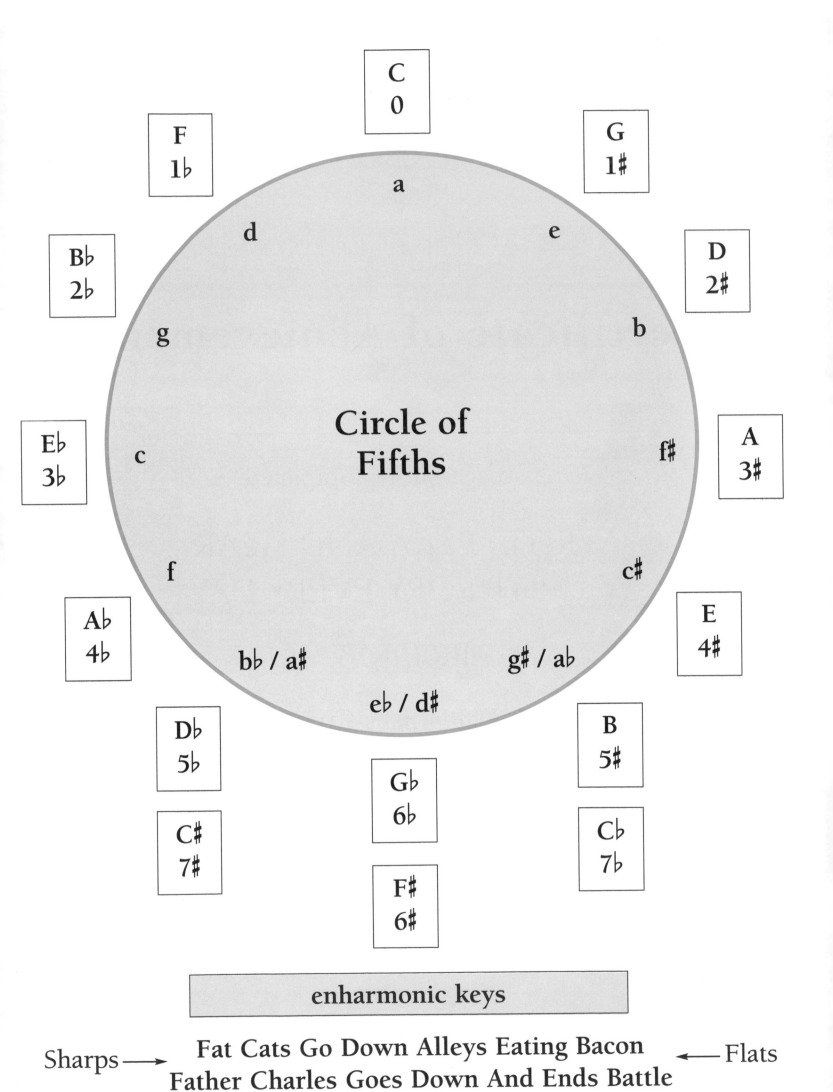

Circle of Fifths

enharmonic keys

Sharps → Fat Cats Go Down Alleys Eating Bacon ← Flats
Father Charles Goes Down And Ends Battle

Certificate of Achievement

_____

has successfully completed

WRITE, PLAY, AND HEAR
YOUR THEORY EVERY DAY®

BOOK 3

of The FJH Pianist's Curriculum.®

You are now ready for Book 4.

_____

Date

_____

Teacher's Signature

FJH2010